CAMBRIDGE LIBRARY COLLECTION

Books of enduring scholarly value

Travel and Exploration

The history of travel writing dates back to the Bible, Caesar, the Vikings and the Crusaders, and its many themes include war, trade, science and recreation. Explorers from Columbus to Cook charted lands not previously visited by Western travellers, and were followed by merchants, missionaries, and colonists, who wrote accounts of their experiences. The development of steam power in the nineteenth century provided opportunities for increasing numbers of 'ordinary' people to travel further, more economically, and more safely, and resulted in great enthusiasm for travel writing among the reading public. Works included in this series range from first-hand descriptions of previously unrecorded places, to literary accounts of the strange habits of foreigners, to examples of the burgeoning numbers of guidebooks produced to satisfy the needs of a new kind of traveller - the tourist.

Narrative of the Proceedings of Pedrarias Davila in the Provinces of Tierra Firme, or Catilla del Or

The publications of the Hakluyt Society (founded in 1846) made available edited (and sometimes translated) early accounts of exploration. The first series, which ran from 1847 to 1899, consists of 100 books containing published or previously unpublished works by authors from Christopher Columbus to Sir Francis Drake, and covering voyages to the New World, to China and Japan, to Russia and to Africa and India. This book, published in 1865, contains an early account of Spanish exploration on and around the Isthmus of Panama. The author accompanied Pedrarias Davila when he was appointed governor of the isthmus in 1514, and his report about the legendary riches of the Inca empire of Peru led to Pizarro's expedition and the destruction of the Inca civilisation. The translator's introductory essay describes the expedition of Balboa, who preceded Davila as governor of the isthmus, and was the first European to see the Pacific Ocean.

T0382555

Cambridge University Press has long been a pioneer in the reissuing of out-of-print titles from its own backlist, producing digital reprints of books that are still sought after by scholars and students but could not be reprinted economically using traditional technology. The Cambridge Library Collection extends this activity to a wider range of books which are still of importance to researchers and professionals, either for the source material they contain, or as landmarks in the history of their academic discipline.

Drawing from the world-renowned collections in the Cambridge University Library, and guided by the advice of experts in each subject area, Cambridge University Press is using state-of-the-art scanning machines in its own Printing House to capture the content of each book selected for inclusion. The files are processed to give a consistently clear, crisp image, and the books finished to the high quality standard for which the Press is recognised around the world. The latest print-on-demand technology ensures that the books will remain available indefinitely, and that orders for single or multiple copies can quickly be supplied.

The Cambridge Library Collection will bring back to life books of enduring scholarly value (including out-of-copyright works originally issued by other publishers) across a wide range of disciplines in the humanities and social sciences and in science and technology.

Narrative of the Proceedings of Pedrarias Davila in the Provinces of Tierra Firme, or Catilla del Or

And of the Discovery of the South Sea and the Coasts of Peru and Nicaragua

PASCUAL DE ANDAGOYA

CAMBRIDGE UNIVERSITY PRESS

Cambridge, New York, Melbourne, Madrid, Cape Town, Singapore,
São Paolo, Delhi, Dubai, Tokyo

Published in the United States of America by Cambridge University Press, New York

www.cambridge.org
Information on this title: www.cambridge.org/9781108010597

© in this compilation Cambridge University Press 2010

This edition first published 1865
This digitally printed version 2010

ISBN 978-1-108-01059-7 Paperback

WORKS ISSUED BY

The Hakluyt Society.

THE NARRATIVE OF

PASCUAL DE ANDAGOYA.

M.DCCC.LXV.

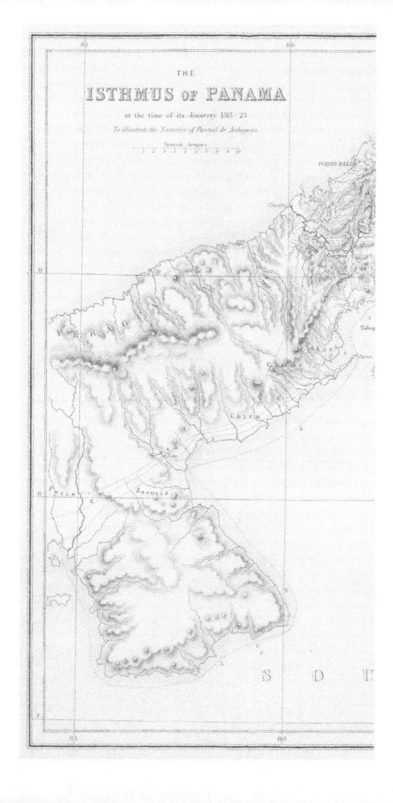

THE
ISTHMUS of PANAMA
at the time of its discovery 1513 - 23
To illustrate the Narrative of Pascual de Andagoya
Spanish leagues

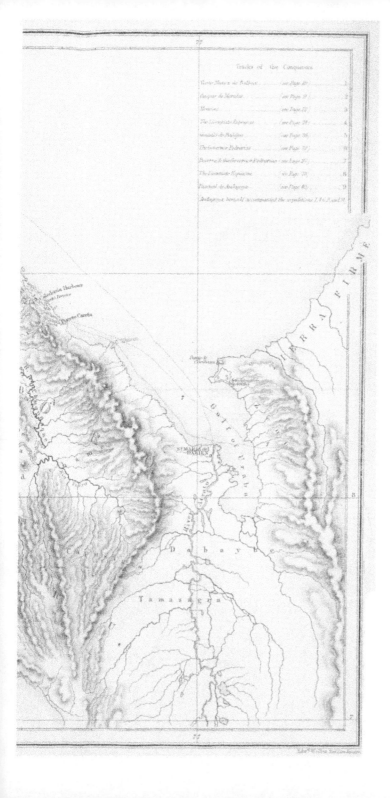

Tracks of the Conquerors

Vasco Nunez de Balboa .... *(see Page 16)* 1

Gaspar de Morales .... *(see Page 19)* 2

Moralez .... *(see Page 22)* 3

The Licentiate Espinosa .... *(see Page 24)* 4

Gonzalo de Badajoz .... *(see Page 36)* 5

The Governor Pedrarias .... *(see Page 39)* 6

Becerra & the Governor Pedrarias ...... *(see Page 39)* 7

The Licentiate Espinosa .... *(see Page 39)* 8

Hurtado de Andagoya .... *(see Page 40)* 9

Andagoya himself accompanied the expeditions 1, 4, 6, 8 and 9.

NARRATIVE OF THE PROCEEDINGS

OF

PEDRARIAS DAVILA

IN THE

PROVINCES OF TIERRA FIRME OR CASTILLA DEL ORO,
AND OF THE DISCOVERY OF THE SOUTH SEA AND
THE COASTS OF PERU AND NICARAGUA.

WRITTEN BY

THE ADELANTADO

PASCUAL DE ANDAGOYA.

TRANSLATED AND EDITED,

WITH NOTES AND AN INTRODUCTION,

BY

CLEMENTS R. MARKHAM.

LONDON:
PRINTED FOR THE HAKLUYT SOCIETY.
M.DCCC.LXV.

INTRODUCTION.

PASCUAL DE ANDAGOYA was one of the officers who accompanied Pedrarias, when he went out as governor of the newly discovered isthmus between the North and South Seas in 1514. Andagoya was engaged in several of the exploring expeditions which were despatched from Darien, and he was the first Spaniard who obtained authentic information respecting the rich empire of the Yncas. His discoveries led to the expeditions of Pizarro and Almagro, and Andagoya himself was eventually governor, for a very short time, of the provinces round Popayan. His narrative is that of an eye-witness of some of the most stirring events which preceded the discovery of Peru. The conquest of the isthmus and the establishment of a colony at Panama were the necessary preliminaries to Spanish dominion along the shores of the South Sea. An account of these events, written by one of the actors in them, therefore, possesses peculiar interest, and the narrative of Pascual de Andagoya[1] has

---

[1] It is printed in the work of Navarrete. *Coleccion de los viages y descrubrimientos, que hicieron por mar los Españoles, desde fines de siglo* xv. *Seccion* iii. *Establicimientos de los Españoles en el Darien.* Tom. iii, No. vii, p. 393. The original MS. is preserved in the Indian Archives at Seville.

accordingly been deemed worthy of a place in the series
of volumes printed for the Hakluyt Society.

A famous discovery had been made, before the arrival of Pedrarias and his train of officers and lawyers,
by one of the greatest men that the age of Spanish
conquest in America produced. Vasco Nuñez de Balboa, in March 1511, found himself the leading and
most popular man in the forlorn colony of Darien.
The expeditions of Nicuesa and Ojeda had failed,
chiefly through the incompetence of their unfortunate
leaders.[1] The man who, a few short months before,
had been a fugitive debtor headed up in a cask, was
now the commander of a great enterprise. An incapable though learned lawyer, the Bachelor Enciso,
alone stood between Vasco Nuñez and his ambition,
and such an obstacle was at once removed. The erudite
author of the *Suma de Geografía* was shipped off to
Spain, and Vasco Nuñez commenced his short but
brilliant career of discovery.

His acts, during his government of the colony of
Darien, stamp him as a born ruler of men. His policy towards the Indians was humane and statesman-like, while
his sympathy for the sufferings of his own men ensured
him just popularity among the wild and reckless spirits
who formed his colony. There is more of diplomacy
and negociation, than of massacre and oppression in
the history of this great discoverer's career; but there
was no want of that dauntless spirit of enterprise, that
resolute endurance of incredible hardships and sufferings by which alone the conquest of the New World

[1] See *note* at p. 34 of my translation of Cieza de Leon.

could be achieved. His treatment of the cacique of
Coiba secured the little colony of Darien a most valuable ally. His visit to the wealthy chief Comogre,
from whose son the first news of the existence of the
great South Sea was received, added another nation to
the list of his allies. His romantic expedition in search
of the golden Dobaybe was unstained by the atrocities
which usually marked the proceedings of Spanish explorers. Finally, his memorable discovery of the Pacific
Ocean could not have been achieved if his humane
diplomacy had not secured the friendship of the Indian
tribes in his rear.

Reduced to the greatest distress by the neglect of
the authorities in Spain and St. Domingo to send him
succour, and surrounded by dense forests and pesti-
lential morasses, Vasco Nuñez never lost heart. He
overcame difficulties which to most men would have
appeared insuperable, and won the proud distinction
of having equalled Cortes and Pizarro in bravery and
perseverance ; while he is among the few *Conquista-
dores* who showed any sign of such qualities as hu-
manity and generosity, when the unfortunate natives
were concerned. Vasco Nuñez fully explained the
difficulties which surrounded him, to the Spanish Government, in a long letter dated January 1513 from
Darien, six months before his discovery of the South
Sea ; and the words of the man himself convey the
best idea of his position. He says :—

" Most Christian and most puissant Lord,

" Some days ago I wrote to your Majesty by a caravel
which came to this town, giving your very Royal Highness

an account of all that has happened in these parts. I also
wrote by a brigantine which left this town for the island of
Española, to let the admiral[1] know that we were in extreme
distress; and now we have been supplied by two ships laden
with provisions. We were then reduced to such extre-
mities that, if succour had been delayed, it would no
longer have been necessary. For no remedy could then
have delivered us from the consequences of famine; and in
our great need we lost 300 of the men we found here of
those I commanded, of those of Uraba under Alonzo de
Ojeda, and of those under Diego de Nicuesa at Veragua.
With much labour I have united all these parties together,
as your Royal Majesty will see in another letter which I
write to your very Royal Highness, where I give an account
of all that has taken place here. I sent, most Royal Highness, to order that the persons who were in the settlement
of Diego de Nicuesa should be brought to this town, and
I treated them with all the attention that was possible.
Your most Royal Highness will be aware that, after Diego
de Nicuesa came to this town and thence departed for
Española, I took as much care of the people that were
left in his settlement, as if they had been under my own
charge, and had been conveyed from Castile by order of
your Royal Highness. When I found that they were in
want, I remembered to send provisions to them one two or
three times, until after a year and a half I conveyed them to
this town, seeing that I should thus further the service of
your most Royal Highness. For if I had not helped them
they would have been lost, five or six dying of hunger every
day, and the survivors being thinned by the Indians. Now
all the men who were left behind by Diego de Nicuesa are
in this town. From the first day of their arrival here they
have been treated as well as if they had been sent by

---

[1] The son of Christopher Columbus, who had inherited that
title, and the government of Hispaniola, from his father.

order of your most Royal Highness, for there has been no difference made with them, any more than if they had come here on the first day. As soon as they arrived here they were given their pieces of land for building and planting in a very good situation, close to those occupied by the men who came with me to this town, for the land was not yet divided, and they arrived in time to receive some of the best pieces. I have to inform your most Royal Highness that both the governors, as well Diego de Nicuesa as Alonzo de Ojeda, performed their duties very ill, and that they were the causes of their own perdition, because they knew not how to act, and because, after they arrived in these parts, they took such presumptuous fancies into their thoughts that they appeared to be lords of the land. They imagined they could rule the land and do all that was necessary from their beds; and thus they acted, believing that they had nothing further to do. But the nature of the land is such that if he who has charge of the government sleeps, he cannot awake when he wishes, for this is a land that obliges the man who governs to be very watchful. The country is difficult to travel through, on account of the numerous rivers and morasses and mountains, where many men die owing to the great labour they have to endure, for every day we are exposed to death in a thousand forms. I have thought of nothing, by day or by night, but how to support myself and the handful of men whom God has placed under my charge, and how to maintain them until your Highness sends reinforcements. I have taken care that the Indians of this land are not ill-treated, permitting no man to injure them, and giving them many things from Castile, whereby they may be drawn into friendship with us. This honourable treatment of the Indians has been the cause of my learning great secrets from them, through the knowledge of which large quantities of gold may be obtained, and your Highness will thus be well served. I have often thought how it will be possible for us to sustain life, seeing that we have been as badly succoured from the island of Española as if we had not been Christians. But our Lord, by his infinite mercy, has chosen to supply us with provisions in this land, though we have often been in such straits that we expected to die of hunger; yet at the time of our greatest necessity our Lord has pointed out the means of relief. Your most Royal Highness must know that after we came here, we were forced to travel from one place to another, by reason of the great scarcity, and it astonishes me how we could have endured such hardships. The things that have happened have been more by the hand of God than by the hand of men. Up to the present time I have taken care that none of my people shall go hence unless I myself go in front of them, whether it be by night or day, marching across rivers, through swamps and forests and over mountains; and your Royal Highness should not imagine that the swamps of this land are so light that they can be crossed easily, for many times we have had to go a league, and two and three leagues, through swamps and water, stripped naked, with our clothes fastened on a shield upon our heads, and when we had come to the end of one swamp we have had to enter another, and to walk in this way from two or three to ten days. And if the person who is entrusted with the government of this land remains in his house, and leaves the work to others, no one else he can send in his place can manage the people so well, or fail to make mistakes which may cause the destruction of himself and of all who are with him. I can say this with truth, as a person that has seen what happens; for sometimes, when I have been unable to go with the men because I have been detained by some business connected with the sowing of the crops, I have observed that those whom I have sent in my place, have not acted according to reason.

"I, my Lord, have taken care that everything that has

been obtained, up to the present day, shall be properly divided, as well the gold and the pearls (the shares of your most Royal Highness being put on one side) as the clothing and eatables; but up to the present time we have valued the eatables more than the gold, for we have more gold than health, and often have I searched in various directions, desiring more to find a sack of corn than a bag of gold; and I can certify the truth of this to your most Royal Highness, for we have been more in want of food than of gold. I assure your most Royal Highness that if I had not personally gone in front of my men, searching for food for those who went with me, as well as for those that remained in this town, there would have been no one left in the town or in the land, unless our Lord had miraculously taken pity upon us. The way I have adopted in dividing the gold that has been procured, is to give a proper share to each man who has been engaged in finding it. All receive shares of the food, although some have not gone in search of it.

" I desire to give an account to your most Royal Highness of the great secrets and marvellous riches of this land of which God has made your most Royal Highness the Lord, and me the discoverer before any other, for which I give many thanks and much praise for all the days of the world, and I hold myself to be the most fortunate man that has been born in the world, seeing that our Lord has been served at my hands rather than at those of another. As so propitious a commencement has been made, I beseech your most Royal Highness that I may be permitted to complete this great enterprise, and I am bold to make this supplication to your most Royal Highness, because I know that you will thus be well served, for I venture to say that, with the help of God, and with industry, I shall be able to conduct the enterprise in such a way that your most Royal Highness will be thereby well served. But for this purpose your most Royal Highness should order that 500 or more men be presently sent from the island of Española, that, united with those already here, although we have not more than 100 fit to bear arms, I may be able to march into the interior of the land, and pass over to the other sea on the south side.

"That which I, by much labour and great hardships, have had the fortune to discover, is as follows :—In this province of Darien many very rich mines have been found, and there is gold in great quantities. Twenty rivers have been discovered, and thirty containing gold flow from a mountain about two leagues from this town, towards the south. This mountain is towards the west, and between the town and the mountain no gold bearing rivers have been seen, but I believe they exist. Following the course of the great river of San Juan for thirty leagues on the right hand side, one arrives at a province called Abanumaqué, which contains much gold. I have certain intelligence that there are very rich rivers of gold in this province, from a son of a Cacique,[1] and from other Indian men and women whom I have taken. Thirty leagues up this great river, on the left hand, a very large and beautiful stream flows into it, and two days' journey up this stream there is a Cacique called Davaive. He is a very great lord with a large and very populous land. He has great store of gold in his house, so much indeed that he who does not know the things of this land would be very hard of belief. I know this of a certainty. All the gold that goes forth from this gulf comes from the house of the cacique Davaive, as well as all that is owned by the caciques of those districts, and it is reported that they have many pieces of gold curiously worked, and very large. Many Indians who have seen them, tell me that this cacique Davaive has certain bags of gold, and that it takes the whole strength of a man to lift one of them on to his back.

"The cacique collects the gold, and this is the manner of his obtaining it.

---

[1] This was the son of the Cacique Comogre. See p. 11 (note).

"Two days' journey from his house there is a very beautiful country inhabited by a very evil Carib race, who eat as
many men as they can get. They are a people without a
chief, and there is no one whom they obey. They are warlike, and each man is his own master. They are lords of
the mines, and these mines, according to the news I have
heard, are the richest in the world. They are in a land
where there is a mountain which appears to be the largest in
the world, and I believe that so large a mountain has never
before been seen. It rises up on the Uraba side of this gulf,
somewhat inland, it may be twenty leagues from the sea.
The way to it is in a southerly direction. At first the land
is flat, but it gradually rises, and at last it is so high that it
is covered with clouds. During two years we have only twice
seen its summit, because it is continually obscured by clouds.
Up to a certain point it is covered with a forest of great trees,
and higher up the mountain has no trees whatever. It rises
in the most beautiful and level country in the world, near the
territory of this cacique Davaive. The very rich mines are
in this land towards the rising of the sun, and it is two days'
journey from the rich mines to the abode of this cacique
Davaive.

"There are two methods of collecting the gold without any
trouble. One is by waiting until the river rises in the
ravines, and when the freshes pass off, the beds remain dry,
and the gold is laid bare, which has been robbed from the
mountains and brought down in very large lumps. The
Indians describe them as being the size of oranges or of a
fist, and others like flat slabs. The other way of gathering
gold is by waiting until the plants on the hills are dry, which
are set on fire, and when they are consumed the Indians go
to search in the most likely places, and collect great quantities of very beautiful grains of gold. The Indians who
gather this gold, bring it in grains to be melted, and barter
it with this cacique Davaive, in exchange for youths and boys

to eat, and for women to serve them as wives, whom they do
not eat.   He gives them also many pigs, as well as fish,
cotton cloth, and salt, and such worked pieces of gold as
they want.   These Indians only trade with the cacique
Davaive, and with no one else.

"This cacique Davaive has a great place for melting gold
in his house, and he has a hundred men continually working
at the gold.   I know all this of a certainty, for I have never
received any other account, in whatever direction I may have
gone.   I have heard it from many caciques and Indians, as
well from natives of the territory of this cacique Davaive, as
from those of other parts, so that I believe it to be true,
because I have heard it in many forms, obtaining the information from some by torments, from others for love, and
from others in exchange for things of Castile.[1]   I also have
certain information that, after ascending this river of San
Juan for fifty leagues there are very rich mines on both sides
of the river.   The river is navigated in the small canoes of
the Indians, because there are many narrow and winding
mouths overhung with trees, and these cannot be passed
except in canoes three or four *palmos* in breadth.   After the
river is entered ships may be built of eight or more *palmos*,
which may be rowed with twenty oars, like *fastas*,[2] but the
river has a very strong current, which even the Indian canoes
can hardly stem.   When it is blowing fresh the vessels may
make sail, assisted by the oars in turning some of the
windings.

"The people who wander along the upper course of this
great river are evil and warlike.   It is necessary to be very
cunning in dealing with them.   I have news of many other

---

[1] The Dobaybe was as famous a person as the El Dorado,
amongst the early Spanish conquerors. He appears to have been
a chief whose territory stretched along the banks of the river
Atrato.

[2] Lateen rigged craft in the Mediterranean.

things, but I will not declare them until I know them more fully, believing that I shall discover them with the help of God.

"That which is to be found down this coast to the westward is the province called Careta, which is twenty leagues distant. There are certain rivers in it which contain gold, according to Indian men and women who are in this town. The Spaniards have not gone there, in order not to rouse the country until we have more men, for we are now few in number. Further down the coast, at a distance of forty leagues from this city, and twelve leagues inland, there is a cacique named Comogre, and another named Pocorosa; who are at equal distances from the sea. They have many wars with each other. They each have a town inland, and another on the sea-coast, by which the interior is supplied with fish. The Indians assured me that there were very rich rivers of gold near the houses of these caciques. At the distance of a day's journey from the cacique Pocorosa's house there are the most beautiful mountains that have been seen in these parts. They are clear of forests, except some groves of trees along the banks of mountain streams.

"In these mountains there are certain caciques who have great quantities of gold in their houses. It is said that these caciques store their gold in *barbacoas* like maize, because it is so abundant that they do not care to keep it in baskets; that all the rivers of these mountains contain gold; and that they have very large lumps in great abundance. Their method of collecting the gold is by going into the water, and gathering it in their baskets. They also scrape it up in the beds of streams, when they are dry; and that your most Royal Highness may be more completely informed concerning these parts, I send an Indian workman of that district who has collected it many times. Your most Royal Highness must not hold this subject as one for a jest, for I am in truth well assured of it by many principal Indians and caciques. I, sire, have myself been very near these mountains, within a day's journey, but I did not reach them, because I was unable to do so, owing to the want of men; for a man gets as far as he can, not as far as he wishes. Beyond these mountains the country is very flat towards the south, and the Indians say that the other sea is at a distance of three days' journey. All the caciques and Indians of the country of Comogre tell me that there is such great store of gold collected in lumps, in the houses of the caciques of the other sea, that we should be astonished. They declare that there is much gold in very large grains in all the rivers of the other coast, and that the Indians of the other sea come to the residence of this cacique Comogre by a river, and bring gold from the mines to be melted, in very large round grains, and in great quantity. In exchange for the gold they get cotton cloth and good looking Indian men and women. They do not eat them like the people towards the great river. They say that the people of the other coast are very good and well mannered; and I am told that the other sea is very good for canoe navigation, for that it is always smooth, and never rough like the sea on this side, according to the Indians. I believe that there are many islands in that sea. They say that there are many large pearls, and that the caciques have baskets of them, as well as the Indian men and women, generally. The river which flows from the territory of the cacique Comogre to the other sea, forms itself into three branches, each one of which enters the other sea by itself. They say that the pearls are brought to the cacique Comogre in canoes by the western branch. The canoes with gold from all parts enter by the eastern branch. It is a most astonishing thing and without equal, that our Lord has made you the lord of this land. It should not be forgotten that your most Royal Highness will be served by sending me reinforcements; when I will, if our Lord favours me, discover things so grand, and places where so much gold and such wealth may be had, that a great part of the world might be conquered with it. I assure your most Royal Highness that I have worked with more diligence for the service of your most Royal Highness than the governors who were lost here, Alonzo de Ojeda and Diego de Nicuesa; for I have not remained in my bed while my people were entering and exploring the country. I must let your most Royal Highness know that no party has gone into any part of this land unless I was in front as a guide opening the road with my own hands, for those who went with me. If this is not believed, I refer to what I have sent home, and to the fruits which each one of those who have laboured here has yielded.

"As one who has seen the things of these parts, and who has more knowledge of the land than anyone else has hitherto acquired, and because I desire that the affairs of these regions which I have originated, may flourish and reach such a position as to be of service to your most Royal Highness; I must make known what is necessary to be done and to be provided at once, and until the land is known and explored. The chief requirement is that a thousand men should come from the island of Española, for those who might come direct from Castile would not be fit for much until they were accustomed to the country, for they would be lost, and us who are now here with them. Your most Royal Highness will please to order that, for the present, this colony be supplied with provisions at the hands of your most Royal Highness, that the land may be explored and its secrets made known. And thus two things will be effected; one that much money will be gained in the markets, and the other and principal one that, the land being supplied with provisions, great things and vast riches may be discovered, by the help of God. It is also necessary to provide the means of building small ships for the rivers, and to send pitch, nails, ropes, and sails, with some master shipwrights

who understand ship-building. Your most Royal Highness
should also send two hundred cross-bows with very strong
stays and fittings, and with long ranges. They should not
weigh more than two pounds; and money would thus be
saved, because each man in this place ought to have one or
two cross-bows, as they are very good arms against the
Indians, and useful in the chase of birds and other game.
Two dozen very good hand-guns, of light metal, are also
required; for those made of iron are soon damaged by the
constant damp, and are eaten away with rust. They should
not weigh more than from twenty-five to thirty pounds, and
they should not be long, so that a man may be able to
carry one of them wherever it may be necessary. Very good
powder is also wanted.

"For the present, it is necessary that as large a rein-
forcement of troops as possible should be sent to the province of Darien, because it is a land very full of hostile
tribes. There should also be a force at the mines of Tubanama, in the province of Comogre, because it is also a
very populous region. At present, most puissant lord, the
troops cannot build with lime and stone, nor with mud,
but are obliged to make double palisades of very strong
wood, with mud between them, surrounded by a good strong
ditch. And those who tell your most Royal Highness that
forts may be built of stone and lime, or of other material,
have not seen the quality of the land. What I would urge,
most puissant lord, is that people should come, so that the
land may be explored from these two stations of Davaive
and Comogre, and that the secrets of it may be known, as
well as those of the sea on the other side towards the south,
and all other matters. Your most Royal Highness should
also send workmen to look after the cross-bows, for every
day they get out of order, owing to the constant damp. In
all the matters which I have named, your most Royal Highness would gain money, and it would cost nothing beyond
the order to send people here.

"Those Indians, in certain of the provinces, who eat men, and others at the bottom of the gulf of Uraba and in the extensive flooded parts near the great river of San Juan and round the gulf, at the entrance of the flat country of the province of Davaive, have no workshops, nor do they support themselves on anything but fish, which they exchange for maize. These are worthless people, and when canoes of Christians have gone on the great river of San Juan, they have come against them, and have killed some of our people. The country where the Indians eat men is very bad and useless, and can never at any time be turned to account. But these Indians of Caribana have richly deserved death a thousand times over, for they are a very evil race, and have killed many of our Christians when we lost the ship. I would not make slaves of so bad a people, but would order them to be destroyed, both old and young, that no memory may remain of them. I speak now of Caribana and for twenty leagues inland, the people being evil, and the country sterile and worthless. And it will be serviceable to your Highness to give permission to take these natives to Española and the other islands occupied by Christians, to be sold and made profitable, that other slaves may be bought for their price; for it is impossible to keep them even for a day, the country being very extensive, where they can run away and hide. Thus the settlers in these parts, not having Indians secured, cannot work for the service of your Highness, nor extract any gold from the mines. The settlers would also beseech your Highness to grant them permission to bring Indians from Veragua, from a gulf called San Blas, which is fifty leagues from this town, down the coast. Your Highness will be well served in granting this request, because it is a very worthless land, covered with great swamps and forests, and, seen from the sea, it appears to be inundated. So that no profit whatever can be made out of these Indians of Veragua and Caribana, except in this way, by bringing them to Christian settlements, whence they can be taken to Cuba, Jamaica, and other islands inhabited by Christians, to be exchanged for other Indians, of which there are many in those islands. Thus by sending the warlike Indians far from their homes, the natives of these parts will labour well in the islands, and those of the islands here. I must inform your Highness that permission to take the Indians of the islands to the main land would be very conducive to your service, and I must make known to your Highness that, for a distance of two hundred leagues round this town there is no inhabited island, except one in Carthagena, where the people defend themselves well.

" As regards the gold that is collected from the Indians by barter or during war, it will conduce to your service to give permission that henceforth a fifth may be given to your Highness of all that may be obtained; and the reason why this will conduce to the service of your Highness is that, the share being a fourth, it is looked upon as hard service to discover land and to march in war through great hardships, for in truth they are so great as to be intolerable. The men prefer to seek for gold, and there are very good mines near here, rather than to go and die. And if I, or the governor who may succeed me, have to make the Christians go inland on expeditions of discovery, they will never go willingly, and a thing done against the will is never so well done as it should be; while, when it is done willingly, all will be done well and according to our desire. I, therefore, assure your Highness that if the Royal share of gold is a fifth, it will be collected in much larger quantity than when it is a fourth, besides which the country will be discovered according to your Highness's desire.

" With respect to the arms and the means of building brigantines, and the shipwrights, these are important points, because without them no good work can be done. If your Highness should order them to be sent, it would be entirely at the cost of the settlers in these parts, without any expense to your Highness; and if your Highness would command that everything should be supplied which I have asked for, it would be a great advantage, and the land would be provided with all that is necessary. Your Highness should receive all this from me as your loyal servant, and should give it credence because your Highness's service will thus be advanced. I do not desire to make towers of wind like the governors whom your Highness sent out, for between them both they have lost eight hundred men, and those whom I have rescued scarcely amount to fifty, and this is the truth. Your Highness will consider all that I have done, and discovered, and endured with these people, without any help but from God and my own industry.

"If I have erred in anything in working for the service of your Highness, I beseech your Highness that my earnest desire to serve your Highness may be considered. Although, most puissant Lord, I have not succeeded in doing all that is necessary in this land, I can certify that I know how to administer better than all those who have come here hitherto: and that your Highness may understand this, you must consider how little other governors have discovered until to-day, and how they have all failed, and left these shores very full of graves, while, although many Christians may lie underground, it is true that most of those that have died have been eaten by dogs and crows. I do not desire to enlarge upon this, but your Highness should know what each man has been able to do and has done up to this time.

"Most puissant Lord,—I have sent Sebastian del Campo, that your Highness may be better informed of all that has passed here; and I entreat your Highness to give him full credence, for he has been informed by me of the whole truth concerning all that can be done in the service of your Highness, and of that which ought to be done for this land.

"Your Highness must know that formerly there were

certain disagreements here, because the alcaldes and regidores of this town, filled with envy and treachery, attempted to seize me, and when they failed in that, they made false charges against me with false witnesses and in secret. I complain of this to your Highness, because if such acts are not chastised, no governor whom your Highness may send here will be free from attacks. For I, being alcalde mayor for your Highness, have been exposed to a thousand slanders; and if the representative of your Highness is not respected, he cannot do what is necessary for your service. And because the alcaldes and regidores sent an accusation against me, which I believe your Highness will see; I appointed two gentlemen as my judges, that they might draw up a report of my life, and of the great and loyal services which I have done for your Highness in those parts of the Indies where we now are; which I send to your Highness, that you may see the malice of these people, and because I believe that your Highness will be pleased with all that I have done in these parts for your service. I beseech your Highness that favour may be shown me in proportion to my services. I also send a report of what passed with respect to those who invented these calumnies.

"Most puissant Lord, I desire to ask a favour of your Highness, for I have done much in your service. It is that your Highness will command that no bachelor of laws nor of anything else, unless it be of medicine, shall come to this part of the Indies on pain of heavy punishment which your Highness shall order to be inflicted, for no bachelor has ever come here who is not a devil, and who does not lead the life of devils. And not only are they themselves evil, but they give rise to a thousand law-suits and quarrels. This order would be greatly to the advantage of your Highness's service, for the country is new. Most puissant Lord, in a brigantine that we sent from here, on board of which was Juan de Quizedo and Rodrigo de Colmenares, I forwarded to your Highness 500 *pesos* of gold from the mines, in very beautiful grains, and as the voyage is somewhat dangerous for small vessels, I now send to your Highness, by Sebastian del Campo, 370 *pesos* of gold from the mines. I would have sent more if it had not been for the impossibility of collecting it during the short time the vessels were here. With respect to all that I have said, I beseech your Highness to do that which is best for your service. May the life and royal estate of your Highness prosper by the addition of many more kingdoms and lordships to your sacred rule, and may all that is discovered in these parts increase the power of your Highness, as your most Royal Highness may desire; for there are greater riches here than in any other part of the world. From the town of Santa Maria del Antigua, in the province of Darien, in the gulf of Uraba, to-day this Thursday the 20th of January in the year 1513. The making and creation of your Highness, who kisses your most royal hands and feet, Vasco Nuñez de Balboa."[1]

This interesting letter gives a clear insight into the position and designs of Vasco Nuñez two years after he had taken command of the colony at Darien. He had headed numerous exploring expeditions, had formed alliances with Indian tribes, and was then preparing his expedition to discover the South Sea, concerning which he had collected correct and detailed information. But his appeal to the king for reinforcements and supplies met with no response, while the crushing

[1] *Navarrete, Coll.*, tom. iii, No. v, p. 375. The original is in the Indian Archives at Seville. Vasco Nuñez addressed another letter to the Emperor, after the arrival of Pedrarias, from which I have quoted in the notes to Andagoya's narrative. It is dated October 16th, 1515.

news was soon afterwards conveyed to him that the
complaints of his enemy, the lawyer Enciso, had been
favourably heard at court, and that he would probably
be summoned to Spain to answer for his conduct.
This intelligence made him resolve to attempt some
great undertaking which might cast oblivion over the
past, and on the 1st of September, 1513, he set out
from Darien, to cross the mountains, and discover the
South Sea.

The details of that famous enterprise are too well
known to require repetition in this place. Had the
news of its successful issue reached the Spanish court
a few months earlier, the fate of half a continent would
have been changed. A young and statesmanlike ruler,
instead of a cruel and passionate old dotard, would
have settled the Isthmus of Panama ; and the humane
and enlightened Vasco Nuñez, instead of the ruthless
and illiterate Pizarro, would have been the conqueror
of Peru. But this was not to be. Vasco Nuñez returned to Darien, from the coast of that mighty ocean
which he had discovered, only to receive the tidings
that old Pedrarias, with fifteen hundred men, was
coming out from Spain to supersede him.

Pedrarias was accompanied by many learned clerks
and gallant knights. Among them were Quevedo the
bishop, Oviedo the future historian, Enciso the learned
geographer and spiteful enemy of Vasco Nuñez, Espinosa the subtle lawyer, Belalcazar the destined conqueror of Quito, Hernando de Soto the discoverer of
the Mississippi, and Pascual de Andagoya.

Andagoya was born in the valley of Cuartango, in the

province of Alava, of good parentage.[1] His father was
a Hidalgo named Juan Ibañez de Arca. He commences
his narrative from the date of his departure from Spain,
in the fleet of Pedrarias, narrates the events of the
voyage, and the arrival of the new governor at Darien,
in the end of July 1514. He then gives a most interesting and valuable account of the manners and customs
of the Indians of the isthmus.[2] This fine race has retained its independence down to the present day. The
unconquerable love of liberty of these Darien Indians
has been favoured by the dense forests, vast swamps, and
inaccessible mountains which form their native land.
The Spanish conquerors, and afterwards the bold Eng-
glish and French buccaneers, traversed the isthmus in
every direction, but modern explorers and surveyors
have been less successful. To this day the narrowest
part of the isthmus, between the Bayanos river and
the Carribean sea, is almost unknown, owing to the
hostility of the Indians.[3] The fullest account of these
people is to be found in the narrative of Lionel Wafer,
a surgeon who served with Dampier, and who lived
amongst them for several months in 1681-82. They
treated him with hospitable kindness, and his truthful
story leaves a most favourable impression of his wild
entertainers. They were probably of the same type as
many kindred tribes that were exterminated by the
ruthless Spaniards, and there can be no doubt that

[1] Navarrete gives a brief biographical notice of Andagoya.
Coleccion, iii, p. 457.

[2] Pages 12 to 18.

[3] See a paper on the Bayanos river by Laurence Oliphant, Esq.,
in the proceedings of the Royal Geographical Society, 1865.

they are a noble and generous race. We are indebted for a very complete knowledge of their characteristics to the narratives of Andagoya and Wafer.[1]

Having given us an account of the Indians, Andagoya relates the proceedings of several exploring expeditions in which he served. His first employment was in the final adventure of the ill-fated Vasco Nuñez. Andagoya was serving with the great discoverer when, with incredible labour, he transported the brigantines, in pieces, over the forest-covered mountains, when he reached the shores of the South Sea for a second time, and when he was recalled by old Pedrarias to be judicially murdered at Acla.[2] After the death of Vasco Nuñez, Andagoya went with the Governor Pedrarias to Panama, and received from him a *repartimiento* of Indians. He married a maid who was in attendance on the governor's wife, and when Panama received the title of a city from Charles V in 1521, Andagoya was appointed one of its first *Regidores*. But he continued to be actively employed with various exploring expeditions, and he gives an account of their proceedings in his narrative. After the founding of Panama he went with the licentiate Espinosa to discover Nicaragua, and returned by land.[3] The unsuccessful expedition of Gonzalo de Badajos, who went down the Bayanos river in 1516, and penetrated beyond Nata, on the Pacific side of the isthmus,[4] was followed by that of Espinosa, in which Andagoya also served.[5] He was

---

[1] *Dampier's Voyages*, iii, p. 344 (3rd edit., London, 1729).
[2] Pages 18 to 22. [3] Pages 24 and 25.
[4] Pages 26 and 27. [5] Pages 28 to 31.

afterwards employed in an expedition to Nicaragua; and he gives a short account of the manners and customs of the Indians of that province.[1]

In 1522 Andagoya was appointed Inspector-General of the Indians on the isthmus, and for the first time took the chief command of an expedition. On this occasion he explored a province called Birú, south of the isthmus, and between the river Atrato and the Pacific. Here he seems to have obtained authentic accounts of the great empire of the Yncas, which, as he tells us, was erroneously called Peru, owing to a confusion between it and this province of Birú where the first tidings concerning it were received. Birú had, however, been already visited in 1515, by Gaspar de Morales and Francisco Pizarro, during their infamous and devastating raid from Darien to the Pearl Islands.[2] Andagoya returned to Panama full of the wonderful news he had collected, but sick from the effects of a ducking which, as he tells us, was so injurious to his health that he was unable to mount a horse for three years afterwards. He was not made of the stern stuff which went to form a conqueror of Peru, and he was easily persuaded by Pedrarias to hand over the undertaking to the partners Pizarro, Almagro, and Luque. He declares, however, that the discovery of Peru was due to the information collected by himself in Birú, and that Pizarro would have fared better if he had more closely followed his instructions.[3] Meanwhile, Andagoya continued to live at Panama, acting as a sort of agent to

[1] Pages 32 to 40.   [2] See pages 9 and 10 (*note*).
[3] Pages 42 and 43.

the Peruvian conquerors. He lost his first wife in 1529
and, as misfortunes seldom come singly, he was, at about
the same time, thrown into prison and afterwards
banished by the new governor of Panama, Pedro de
los Rios. He retired to the island of San Domingo,
where he married his second wife Doña Mayora Mejia.
In 1534 he returned with her to Panama, was appointed
lieutenant to the new governor, Don Francisco de Bar-
rionuevo, and acquired considerable wealth by acting
as agent to Pizarro. In 1536 his *residencia*[1] was taken
with great severity by the licentiate Pedro Vasquez, and
he was sent to Spain, but he was eventually acquitted
and honoured with favours by the Emperor, for his long
and faithful services.

After relating his own adventures in Birú, Andagoya
devotes several pages to an account of the conquest of
Peru, and of the civilisation of the Yncas.[2] His version
of the oft-told tale is valuable, because, from his position,
he must have derived his information from men who
were actually engaged in the events which he described,
and who saw Peru in the first years of the Conquest.

Andagoya happened to be at the Spanish court in
1538, when news arrived of the death of the licentiate
Gaspar de Espinosa at Cuzco, who had been appointed
Governor of New Castille.[3] The government of this
territory was, therefore, granted to Andagoya. He
embarked from San Lucar with sixty men early in
1539, with the title of Adelantado, and reached Panama,

[1] See note at pages 85 and 86 of my translation of the life of
Don Alonzo Enriquez, for an account of these *residencias*.
[2] See pages 42 to 59.   [3] See page 59 (*note*).

where he collected two hundred followers, and made preparations for his expedition down the coast. His new government was to extend along the Pacific coast from the gulf of San Miguel on the isthmus to the river of San Juan; but, unfortunately, its inland boundary was not defined. The geography of the vast regions of South America was little understood in Spain, and grants of the government of territories were often made which over-lapped each other, and created disputes that could only be settled by the strongest arm and most unscrupulous head. So it was that the honest but weak Andagoya found himself opposed to a rough and determined antagonist, the famous Sebastian de Belalcazar, and, as was inevitable, came off second best in the encounter.

Belalcazar was an adventurer who had come to the new world in the train of Pedrarias, and had after-wards followed the fortunes of Pizarro. The conqueror of Peru despatched him with a hundred and forty men to occupy Quito in 1533, and he afterwards marched north, conquering Pasto and Popayan, and reaching Bogota in 1538.[1] He then proceeded to the Spanish court, to petition for a grant of the government of Po-payan and the surrounding provinces, leaving small Spanish colonies in the towns he had founded at Cali, Pasto, Popayan, and a few other places.

Andagoya says that Belalcazar set out for Spain, be-cause he heard that Espinosa had been appointed go-vernor of the territory which he had discovered. As Andagoya had been appointed to succeed Espinosa, he

[1] For an account of Belalcazar, see my translation of Cieza de Leon, p. 110 (*note*).

thus tries to insinuate that Belalcazar knew that the right was not on his side.[1]

Meanwhile the Adelantado Andagoya, with a grant of the Pacific coast from the river San Juan to the isthmus, and with a government having no defined limit inland, was preparing his expedition at Panama. Andagoya left his brother-in-law, Alonzo de Peña, at San Domingo, who was to collect more troops, horses, and stores. He was not long in following his chief with a hundred and forty men, forty horses, ammunition, and supplies, which were conveyed from Nombre de Dios to Panama, and embarked on board a galleon, a caravel, and two brigantines. Andagoya then commenced his voyage along the coast, on February 15th, 1540. He gives a short account of the events of the voyage in his narrative, and of the discovery of the port of Buenaventura, where he landed.[2] Here he heard that there was a town founded by Belalcazar in the interior, called Lili or Cali, and he marched to it at once, over one of the most difficult routes in South America.[3] In this proceeding he was unquestionably encroaching on the discoveries of another man, and Herrera observes that he had a commission to conquer the country round the river San Juan, but that he marched to Cali without considering that there is no river San Juan in that neighbourhood.[4] Yet he arrived at a most opportune moment. The horrible atrocities

---

[1] See page 62.

[2] See page 96. For a further account of the port of Buenaventura, see my translation of Cieza de Leon, chap. xxix.

[3] Page 61.   [4] *Herrera*, dec. iv, lib. v, cap. iii.

of Belalcazar and his followers had driven the Indians to desperation, and they had at length rushed to arms. Timana and Popayan were closely besieged by them, and the Spaniards had been defeated in the open field. Andagoya restored peace to these provinces, established himself at Popayan, and immediately began to busy himself in conciliating and converting the natives. His narrative contains a very curious account of his proceedings during his brief tenure of office.[1]

While Andagoya was thus quietly taking possession of the fruits of the labours of Belalcazar, that bold conqueror was successfully urging his suit at court. Charles V granted him the government of Popayan with the title of Adelantado, chiefly with a view to checking the ambition of the Pizarros in Peru. The new governor went out to Panama, fitted out an expedition, and sailed down the coast to Buenaventura, in the wake of Andagoya. The latter had left one of his followers in command at that port, named Juan Ladrillero, "a man of intelligence in affairs both by land and sea." A conference took place between Belalcazar and Ladrillero, and the new Adelantado was allowed to land without opposition, and to march towards Cali. Andagoya prepared to resist, but some friars and leading citizens interposed, and it was agreed that they should decide upon the rival claims of the two Adelantados. The assembly declared in favour of Belalcazar, who immediately arrested Andagoya, and sent him in chains to Popayan.[2]

[1] See pages 63 to 75.
[2] See my translation of Cieza de Leon, p. 105.

In March 1541 Alonzo de Peña arrived at Buenaventura with the wife and family of the unfortunate Andagoya, and additional supplies and reinforcements. While this officer was endeavouring, by mild and temperate expostulation, to induce the stern Belalcazar to liberate his brother-in-law, the Licentiate Vaca de Castro opportunely arrived at the port. This functionary had been sent out to co-operate with Pizarro in restoring tranquillity to Peru, and, after a tedious voyage, he was glad to land at Buenaventura, resolving to perform the rest of the journey by land. He was very ill from the effects of the hardships he had experienced during his voyage, and was carried to Cali in a chair, on the backs of Indians. He conferred with Belalcazar and his prisoner Andagoya, but was unable to reconcile them; and, having received the astounding tidings of the assassination of Pizarro while he was at Popayan, he continued his journey towards the scene of his duties in Peru, in August 1541. His parting advice was that Andagoya should be sent to Spain, where the Emperor might decide the limits of his government.

At last Belalcazar allowed his rival to set out for Buenaventura, accompanied by his brother-in-law Alonzo de Peña. At the port he received the melancholy news of the death of his wife and children from fever. Leaving one Payo Romero as his lieutenant there, he embarked for Panama, and proceeded thence to Spain; having lost his government, and upwards of 50,000 *castellanos de oro*, besides 20,000 that he had borrowed,—equal to more than £140,000 of our money. His lieutenant Payo Romero was a brutal soldier whose career of rapine and murder was put a stop to, by a revolt of the long-suffering Indians.[1]

The Adelantado Pascual de Andagoya, after he had arranged his affairs in Spain in the best way he could, returned to the Indies in 1546 with the Licentiate Pedro de la Gasca, who was sent out with full powers to put an end to the civil discord caused by the ambition of Gonzalo Pizarro in Peru. Andagoya eventually reached the port of Manta, in the fleet of Gasca, where death closed his eventful career.

He was a brave and honest officer, but he lacked that reckless audacity and self-reliance which were essential for success in those rough and lawless times. Thus Pizarro forestalled him in the discovery of Peru, and he never stood a chance against the bold and unscrupulous Belalcazar, in the struggle for the government of Popayan. The historian Oviedo, who knew him well during the early days of the Darien colony, speaks of him as a noble-minded and virtuous person. He was a man of some education, and his humane treatment of the Indians entitles his name to honourable mention in any history of Spanish conquest in South America. The contrast between his conduct to the natives, and that of Belalcazar, is most striking.

The personal narrative of such an eye witness of some of the leading events which led to the discovery and conquest of Peru, is certainly a most valuable addition to our knowledge of those stirring times.

[1] See my translation of Cieza de Leon, p. 107.

Narrative of the Proceedings

OF

PEDRARIAS DAVILA

IN THE PROVINCES OF TIERRA FIRME OR CASTILLA DEL ORO,

AND OF WHAT HAPPENED IN THE DISCOVERY OF THE SOUTH SEA, AND

THE COASTS OF PERU AND NICARAGUA.

WRITTEN BY THE

ADELANTADO

PASCUAL DE ANDAGOYA.

NARRATIVE

PASCUAL DE ANDAGOYA.

IN the year 1514 Pedrarias de Avila, who had been appointed governor of the mainland called Castilla del Oro,[1]

[1] Pedrarias was among the candidates for the appointment of governor
of Darien, and received it through the favour of the bishop of Burgos.
" He was an elderly man, of rank and high connections, of much repute
in war, having served with honour in Africa. From his feats in the
tournament he had acquired the name of *justador* (the jouster)." He
was a suspicious, fiery, arbitrary old man. *Helps*, i, p. 374.

Vasco Nuñez, in a letter to the king, dated October 16th, 1515, thus
describes Pedrarias. "With respect to the governor, although an honourable person, your highness must know that he is very old for this country, and that he is very ill of a serious disease, insomuch that he has not
been well for a single day since he arrived. He is excessively impatient,
and is a man that would not care much if half his followers were lost.
He has never punished the evil deeds and murders that have been committed both on caciques and Indians by those who have invaded the
country. He is a man who is much pleased to see discord between one
and another, and when it does not exist, he causes it by speaking evil to
one man of another. He gives little credit to what any one says, except
to such an one as he believes to have an interest in speaking the truth.
He takes little heed of the interest of your Majesty, and is a man in whom
reigns all the envy and avarice in the world. He is very miserable if he
sees that there is friendship between respectable people, and is pleased to
hear gossip amongst his followers. He is a man who more easily believes
evil things than good, or those that may be profitable. He is a person
without any judgment, and without any genius for government." Vasco
Nuñez was writing under a strong feeling of disgust at the wretched
misrule which this old incapable had produced : yet the acts of Pedrarias

B

by the Catholic king of glorious memory, embarked at
Seville, with nineteen ships and fifteen hundred men—the
most distinguished company that had yet set out from
Spain.[1] The first land of the Indies at which he arrived
was the island of Dominica. This island has a very large
and beautiful harbour.[2] The land is for the most part hilly
and wooded. Here he disembarked with his troops, and
desired to find out whether there were any inhabitants.
Some of the Spaniards, entering the woods, met with
Indians armed with poisoned arrows, who were wandering
about in the forests which surrounded the camp, watching
for an opportunity to kill a stray Spaniard. These Indians

show that the character thus sketched by an enemy was but slightly
exaggerated. *Navarrete Coll.*, p. 384.

[1] Pedrarias was accompanied by a bishop of the new colony named
Juan de Quevedo, Gaspar de Espinosa as alcalde mayor, the Bachiller
Enciso as alguazil mayor (an old enemy of Vasco Nuñez), and Gonzalvo
Hernandez de Oviedo, the famous historian, as veedor or inspector of
gold foundries. Oviedo afterwards resided with his wife and family in
Hispaniola, paying occasional visits to Spain. In 1526 he published his
Sumario, and in 1535 his *Historia General de las Indias*, which contains
a detailed account of the Darien expedition of Pedrarias. The first part
is published in the collection of Ramusio.

[2] Dominica was discovered by Columbus during his second voyage, in
1493. Dr. Chanca, the physician to the fleet of Columbus, in his letter
to the chapter of Seville, says :—" On Sunday, the 3rd of November, we
saw lying before us an island, and soon on the right hand another appeared : the first was high and mountainous on the side nearest to us ;
the other flat and very thickly wooded. As soon as it became lighter,
other islands began to appear on both sides, so that on that day there
were six islands to be seen lying in different directions, and most of them
of considerable size. We directed our course towards that which we had
first seen" (Dominica, so called from having been discovered on a
Sunday), " and reaching the coast, we proceeded more than a league in
search of a port where we might anchor, but without finding one. All
that part of the island which we could observe, appeared mountainous,
very beautiful, and green even up to the water, which was delightful to
see, for at that season there is scarcely anything green in our own country.
One vessel remained all that day seeking for a harbour, and at length
found a good one, where they saw both people and dwellings."

are a warlike people. They eat human flesh, and both men and women go about stark naked. This island has not been occupied, because the conquest would be very dangerous, and of little value.[1]

Thence, continuing his way to the mainland, Pedrarias arrived at the province of Santa Martha, where he landed all his men. He wished to learn the secrets of the land, and a company of his troops came to a village deserted by its inhabitants, where they captured some spoil, and found a certain quantity of gold in a tomb. The people of this land are almost the same as those of Dominica, they are armed with arrows, and the arrows are poisoned.[2] Here they found certain cloths and the seats on which the devil sat. He was figured on them in the form in which he appeared to the people, and although they did not worship him, as being a thing which appeared to and conversed with them, they noted his form, and represented it on their cloths. Thence Pedrarias sailed for Tierra Firme, without stopping anywhere except at Isla Fuerte, which is in front of Carthagena. The Indians get their salt from this island, and a great number of bags of salt were found. Continuing his voyage, he arrived at a province called Darien, which is at the end of the gulf of the same name. Here he found a certain quantity of Spaniards, who had Vasco Nuñez de Balboa for their captain and alcalde mayor.[3] Their setttlement was

[1] The possession of the island was long disputed between Spaniards, French, and English; but in 1759 it finally became an English colony.

[2] See chapter vii of my translation of *Cieza de Leon*, which treats of "how the barb is made so poisonous with which the Indians of Santa Martha have killed so many Spaniards." Castellanos says that these Indians were called Caribs (or Cannibals), not because they ate human flesh, but because they defended their houses well.

"No porque alli comiesen carne humana
Mas porque defendian bien su casa."
Elegias, pt. ii, canto 3.

[3] When Pedrarias arrived in the gulf of Urabia, he sent a messenger

on the banks of a river, a league and a half from the sea. A
year before these people arrived at that province, the captains Diego de Nicuesa and Alonzo de Ojeda departed from
San Domingo, each one with his fleet. Ojeda went to the
coasts of Paria and Santa Martha, where most of his people
perished in the wars with the Indians or from disease.
The survivors took Francisco Pizarro, who was afterwards
governor of Peru, as their captain or leader, and followed
the coast until they reached Darien, where they established
themselves, and sent a ship to San Domingo, with the news
of what had happened. The judges who were there, appointed the said Vasco Nuñez as alcalde mayor. Diego de
Nicuesa went with his fleet to the coast of Veragua, where
he was lost.[1] Leaving the remainder of his people on a hill

to inform Vasco Nuñez of his arrival, who found the great discoverer in
a cotton shirt, loose drawers, and sandals, helping some Indians to thatch
a house. Vasco Nuñez sent back to say that the colonists were ready to
receive the new governor. The colony consisted of 450 soldiers, while
Pedrarias had a force of nearly 1500 men. On June 30th, 1514, Pedrarias landed at Darien, and, as Herrera tells us (dec. i, lib. ix, cap. 3),
treated Vasco Nuñez in a most malicious manner, appointing his old
enemy Enciso to hold his *Residencia*, fining him several thousand *castellanos*, and for some time keeping him in confinement.

[1] For an account of the proceedings of Ojeda and Nicuesa see my
translation of Cieza de Leon (*note* at p. 34).

In a letter to the king, dated from Darien January 20th, 1513, Vasco
Nuñez says:—" We have lost three hundred men of those I commanded,
of those under Alonzo de Ojeda, and of those under Diego de Nicuesa.
With much labour I have united all these parties together. I sent to
order that all the people who were in the settlement of Diego de Nicuesa
should be brought to this town, and I treated them with all the attention
that was possible. If I had not helped them they would have been lost,
five or six dying every day, and the survivors being thinned by the
Indians. Now all the men who were left behind by Diego de Nicuesa
are in this town. From the first day of their arrival here they have been
as well treated as if they had been sent by order of your most Royal
Highness; for there has been no difference made with them, any more
than if they had come here on the first day. As soon as they arrived
here they were given their pieces of land for building and planting, in
good situations, close to those occupied by the men who came with me

called the hill of Nicuesa, where Nombre de Dios stands, he took a brigantine with some of his men, not knowing where to go, the whole coast being marshy, covered with forest, unhealthy, and thinly peopled. He sailed along the coast in search of the people left by Ojeda, and to discover some country where he might settle, for the coast of Veragua as far as Darien was under his jurisdiction. Ojeda had received the other coast of Santa Martha and Carthagena. Having arrived at Darien, he found Vasco Nuñez and his followers, who received him as a stranger, and would neither give him provisions, nor receive him as their governor. Not desiring to let him remain with them, they made him embark in a boat with some sailors, and it is even said that this boat was caulked with a blunt tool only. I heard this from the caulker himself who did the work.[1] Thus the said

to this town; for the land was not yet divided, and they arrived in time to receive some of the best pieces. I have to inform your most royal highness that both the governors, as well Diego de Nicuesa as Alonzo de Ojeda, performed their duties very ill, and that they were the causes of their own perdition, because they knew not how to act, and because, after they arrived in these parts, they took such presumptuous fancies into their heads that they appeared to be lords of the land. They imagined that they could rule the land and do all that was necessary from their beds, and they acted thus, believing they had nothing further to do. But the nature of the land is such that, if he, who has charge of the government, sleeps, he cannot awake when he wishes; for it is a land that obliges him who governs to be very watchful. For this reason the people desired to be rid of men who did not care whether things went well or ill, like Diego de Nicuesa. This was the cause of the ruin both of the one governor and of the other. These governors believed that they could treat the people as slaves, and they never gave an account of the gold they took, nor of anything else; for which reason all became so careless that, even when they saw gold, they did not care to take it, knowing that they would themselves receive a very small share of it." *Navarrete Coll.*, tom. iii, Num. iv, p. 358.

[1] Spanish carpenters and caulkers call their tools *fierros* or *herramientas*. In caulking seams the *estopa* or oakum is first driven well in with a thin edged caulking iron, and then *remachado* or secured with a blunt one or *fierro grueso*. When Andogoya says that the vessel of Nicuesa was caulked with a blunt tool (*calafateado con ferro groso*), he implies that

Nicuesa was lost, and it was never known what became of him.[1] When the people, whom he had left in Nombre de Dios, found that their captain did not return, obliged by necessity, they followed him, and, arriving at Darien, submitted to the authority of the others.

The Admiral Colon discovered these coasts, both the one and the other.[2]

Pedrarias arrived at Darien in the end of July of the said year 1514, where he was received by the people who were there, and where he landed all his troops. The settlement was small, and there were few resources in the land. The provisions which were on board the ships were disembarked, and divided amongst all the people. The flour and other stores were injured by the sea, and this, added to the evil nature of the land, which is woody, covered with swamps, and very thinly inhabited, brought on so much sickness among the people, that they could not be cured, and in one month seven hundred men died of sickness and hunger. Our arrival weighed so much on those who were already settled at Darien, that they would do no act of charity for any one. As in united enterprises, until experience has shown the way, the correct method of acting is very seldom adopted, so now Pedrarias was appointed jointly with the

the previous operation of driving the oakum well in with a sharp one had been neglected, and that therefore the seams were easily forced open afterwards.

[1] Oviedo says that the last words he was heard to utter as he left the shore were—*Ostende faciem tuam et salvi erimus* ("Show thy face, O Lord, and we shall be saved"). Quoted by *Helps*, i, p. 133.

He set sail on March 1st, 1511, with seventeen faithful companions.

[2] This was in his memorable fourth voyage in 1502. Columbus first sighted the coast a few leagues to the east of the gulf of Honduras, and on September 14th rounded the Cape, which he called *Gracias a Dios*, in search of a strait. He sailed along the coasts of the Mosquito, Costa Rica, and Veragua, and reached a harbour in November, which he called Porto Bello. He went on for eight leagues to the point since named Nombre de Dios, and returned thence to Veragua. He thus discovered the whole coast from the gulf of Honduras nearly to that of Darien.

bishop and officers (without whom he could do nothing). These, seeing how the people were dying, began to send out captains in various directions, not to make settlements, but to bring as many Indians as possible to Darien.[1] They seldom succeeded, but lost many of their people in fights with the Indians, some returning defeated, and others with prisoners. As there were so many voices in every measure, each one given from motives of interest or wilfulness, neither was good order preserved, nor was any evil doer punished.[2]

It was but a short time since Vasco Nuñez had reached a point near the South Sea, whence he had seen it. The captains and troops who went forth in that direction, where the country is healthier and more thickly peopled, brought back great troops of captive natives in chains, and all the gold they could lay their hands on. This state of things continued for nearly three years. The captains divided the captive Indians amongst the soldiers, and brought the gold to Darien. They gave each man his share. To the bishop,

[1] The first expedition sent out by Pedrarias was commanded by Juan de Ayora, who was ordered to build fortresses on the territories of the caciques Comogre, Pocorosa, and Tubanamá. He obtained gold by torturing and burning the Indians, and then sailed away with it, and was never heard of again in Darien. One Bartolomé Hurtado was despatched in search of Ayora, and brought back a hundred Indians as slaves, many of whom he gave away as bribes to the principal officials in Darien.

[2] Vasco Nuñez wrote a letter to the king, dated October 16th, 1515, in which he begged that some one might be sent to examine into the state of the colony. He declared that he who would bring it back into the condition it once was in, must neither sleep nor be careless. He said that the Indians, who were formerly like sheep, had become as fierce lions. That while once they used to come out in the roads with presents for the Christians, they now go forth to kill them. He explained that this change had been caused by the evil treatment they had received from the captains who had invaded their territories, killed many chiefs and Indians without any reason, and stolen their women and children. The crimes of these captains had remained unpunished, while there is not a single friendly tribe left, except the cacique of Careta, who remained neutral, because of his proximity to Darien.

the officers who had a voto in the government, and the
governor, they gave a share of the Indians; and, as they
were appointed as captains by the favour of those who
governed, from among their relations and friends, although
they had committed many evil deeds, none were punished.
In this manner the land suffered for a distance of more than
a hundred leagues from Darien. All the people who were
brought there, and there was a great multitude, were immediately sent to the gold mines, for they were rich in that
land; and as they came from a great distance, and were
worn out and broken down by the great burdens they had
to carry, and as the climate was different from their own,
and unhealthy, they all died. In these transactions the
captains never attempted to make treaties of peace, nor
to form settlements, but merely to bring Indians and gold to
Darien, and waste them there.

About thirty leagues from Darien there was a province
called Careta,[1] and another, at a distance of five leagues

[1] " To the westward of Darien is a province called Careta, which is
about twenty leagues distant. There are certain rivers in it which contain gold, according to Indian men and women who are in this town."
Letter of Vasco Nuñez.

It would appear that Careta was the name of the cacique, and that
the province was called Coiba. Careta had hospitably entertained two
Spanish fugitives from Nicuesa's party, who fled to Darien, and basely
proposed to Vasco Nuñez the invasion of their benefactor's territory.
Accordingly Vasco Nuñez marched to Coiba with 130 armed men, and
was received most hospitably. He feigned to return to Darien, but in
the dead of night he suddenly attacked the village, and took Careta and
his family prisoners, seizing provisions enough to load two brigantines.
Careta, when brought to Darien, offered his daughter to Vasco Nuñez
as a pledge of his friendship if he was set at liberty, and the invader
allowed him to depart. Vasco Nuñez fell in love with Careta's daughter,
and retained an unswerving attachment for her to the day of his death.
He kept his word with her father, and invaded the country of his enemy
the cacique of Ponca. When Vasco Nuñez set out, on September 1st,
1513, to discover the South Sea, he sailed from Darien to Coiba, the
territory of his lady love's father, the cacique Careta, who furnished him
with guides and warriors. Careta always remained a firm ally of his
quasi son-in-law.

from it, called Acla. In these two provinces there were two lords who were brothers, and, one of them desiring to possess all, there were great wars, so that a battle was fought in a place called Acla, where Pedrarias afterwards established a town of Christians. Before the battle this place had another name; for Acla, in the language of that land, means "*the bones of men*," and the province retained that name because of the quantity of bones strewn on the battle field.[1] After this war there was so small a number of Indians, that when we arrived they made no resistance. These people were more civilised than those of the coast of Santa Martha; for the women were very well dressed, in embroidered cotton mantles which extended from the waist downwards, and they slept on beds of the same material. These dresses of the women reached down so as to cover the feet, but the arms and bosom were uncovered. The men went about with their private parts covered with a bright coloured sea shell very well carved, which was secured round the loins by cords. In this way they were able to run and walk with great freedom.[2] These shells were used as articles of barter with the inner lands, for they were not found any where except on the sea coast. The land is covered with forest, like that of Darien, though it is more healthy, and there are gold mines in many parts of it.

At this time a captain named Gaspar de Morales set out to discover the South Sea, and he went out on it as far as the islands of Pearls, where the lord was friendly, and gave him rich pearls. He was the first man who visited them.[3]

---

[1] Don Alonzo Enriquez de Guzman says : " I sailed from the island of Hispaniola on my way to Peru, and arrived at the port of Nombre de Dios, in the province of Castilla del Oro. The native name of the place means *Bones*, and it was so called on account of the number of people who have died there. See my *Translation*, p. 88.

[2] *Sin que por ninguna via se les pareciese cosa alguna de su natura, salvo los genetivos, que estos no cabian en el caracol.*

[3] Morales was sent to the South Sea in search of pearls, with eighty

The first province to the westward of Acla is Comogre,[1] where the country begins to be flat and open. From this

Spaniards,   He was received in a friendly manner, and was given many valuable pearls. On his return he murdered the Indians, stole their women, and caused twenty chiefs to be torn to pieces by his dogs. Vasco Nuñez says :—" He committed greater cruelties than have ever been heard of among Arabs, Christians, or any other people. He killed a hundred women and young lads, and all this, most puissant Lord, has passed without any punishment. On the island he burnt the houses and the stores of corn, but, nevertheless, the cacique gave him 15 or 16 marcs of pearls, and 4,000 *pesos de oro*. He afterwards seized many Indian men and women on this rich island, and sold them as slaves at Darien, without any conscience." He adds that Morales brought a pearl from the rich island which weighed ten *tomines*, very perfect and without a flaw, and of so beautiful a lustre and shape as to be fit for the King's use." *Navarrete Coll.*, p. 379. Morales seems to have been hard pressed during his retreat, by the outraged Indians, whose women and children he was taking away, to sell at Darien. He murdered these captives one by one, and left their bodies in the road, in the hope of thus checking the pursuit of the Indians.

Francisco Pizarro served as second in command, in this infamous expedition of Morales. The invaders entered the territory of the Cacique Biru, whose name supplied the Spaniards with an erroneous designation for the great Empire of the Yncas. It was here, possibly, that Pizarro first heard faint rumours respecting the scene of his future conquest, and here Andagoya afterwards collected fuller information on the same subject.

[1] " Forty leagues down the coast, from the city of Darien, and twelve leagues inland, there is a cacique named Comogre, and another named Pocorosa, who are at equal distances from the sea. They have many wars with each other. They each have a town inland, and another on the sea coast, by which the interior is supplied with fish. The Indians assured me that there were very rich rivers of gold near the houses of these caciques. At the distance of a day's journey from the cacique Pocorosa's house there are the most beautiful mountains. They are clear of forest, except some groves of trees along the banks of the streams. In these mountains there are certain caciques who have great quantities of gold in their houses. It is said that these caciques store their gold in *barbacoas*, like maize, because it is so abundant that they do not care to keep it in baskets. Their method of collecting the gold is by going into the water and gathering it in their baskets. They also scrape it up in the beds of streams when they are dry : and that your Royal Highness may be more completely informed concerning these parts, I send an

point forward the country was populous, though the chiefs were of small account, being from a league to two leagues apart from each other. In this country there is a province called Peruqueta, extending from one sea to the other, and including the Pearl Islands and the gulf of San Miguel. And another province, which was called the land of confusion, because there was no chief in it, is also called Cueva. The people are all one, speaking one language, and are dressed like those of Acla. From this province of Peruqueta to Adechame, a distance of forty leagues still in a westerly direction, the country is called Coiba, and the language is the same as that of Cueva, only more polished, and the people have more self-assertion. They differ also in the men not wearing the shells, like those of Cueva; for they go quite naked, without any covering. The women are

Indian workman of that district, who has collected it many times. I, Sire, have myself been very near these mountains, within a day's journey, but I did not reach them because I was unable, for a man gets as far as he can, not as far as he wishes. Beyond these mountains the country is very flat towards the south, and the Indians say that the other sea is at a distance of three days' journey. All the caciques and Indians of the country of Comogre tell me that there is such great store of gold collected in lumps, in the houses of the caciques of the other sea, that we should be astonished. They declare that the Indians of the other sea come to the residence of this cacique Comogre by a river, and bring gold to be melted. In exchange for the gold they get cotton cloth, and good looking Indian men and women. They do not eat these men and women, like the people towards the great river" (Atrato). " The river which flows from the territory of the cacique Comogre to the other sea forms itself into three branches, each of which enters the other sea by itself. Pearls are brought to the cacique Comogre to be exchanged, by the western branch ; and the canoes with gold enter by the eastern branch." *Letter of Vasco Nuñez to the King.* I presume this must be the river Chucunaque of the Spanish maps.

Vasco Nuñez had formed a friendship with the cacique of Comogre, before the arrival of Pedrarias, and had visited his house, which was, according to Las Casas, 150 feet long, 80 broad, and 80 in height. Comogre gave the Spaniards some gold, over the division of which they quarrelled, and then it was that his son told them of a country abounding in gold, far to the south. It has been supposed that the young man

adorned like those of Acla and Cueva. From these provinces most of the Indians were taken, who were brought to
Darien, for as they were the nearest and most populous, no
sooner had one captain returned from them, than another
set out.

One of the captains of Pedrarias, named Meneses, established a settlement called Santa Cruz, in the territory of
a chief named Pocorosa, in the province of Cueva, on the
north sea. From this settlement he advanced into the
province of Cueva with part of his forces, and was defeated
by the Indians, several of his people being killed. Then,
seeing that the Spaniards in Santa Cruz were defeated and
reduced in numbers, the Indians attacked them, and killed
them all, so that no one remained alive except a woman, whom
the chief took for himself, and lived with as his wife for
several years. His other wives, being zealous that the chief
liked her better than them, killed her, and gave their lord
to understand that an alligator had eaten her, when she went
to bathe in the river. Thus this settlement was destroyed.

In these provinces there were no large villages, but each
chief had three or four houses or more on his land. These
were close together, and each man built his house in the
place where he sowed his crop. The chiefs in these provinces were of small account, because there were many of
them, and they had great disputes concerning their fishing
and hunting grounds, in which many were killed. The
country is very beautiful. The chiefs, in their language, are
called *Tiba*, and the principal men of the family of a chief
are called *Piraraylos*. The brave men renowned in war,
who had killed an adversary, or had come wounded from the
battle, received the name *Cabra*, as their title. The people

alluded to the empire of the Yncas, but I consider it very improbable
that he ever heard of that distant land. It is far more likely that he
alluded to some of the districts where there were gold washings, near the
southern frontier of his father's territory. He, however, undoubtedly
gave Vasco Nuñez the first notice concerning the Pacific Ocean.

lived according to natural laws of justice, without any ceremonies or worship.   The chiefs, in these provinces, settled
disputes in person, and there were no other judges or officers, except those who apprehended prisoners.   Their manner of judging was this :—The parties appeared, and each
stated the facts of the case.   Then, without evidence from
witnesses, and holding it for certain that the parties would
speak the truth (for he who lied to a chief was put to
death), the suit was determined, and there was no further
dispute respecting it. In these provinces the chiefs received
no rent nor tribute from their subjects, except personal service ; but whenever a chief wished to build a house, sow
a crop, procure fish, or wage war, every one had to assist
without receiving any reward beyond food and drink, and
thus they neither exacted anything from their people, nor
did they want for anything.   They were feared and loved,
and the gold they possessed was either obtained by barter,
or dug out of mines by the Indians.   They had laws and
regulations by which he who killed another, or committed
robbery, was put to death.   No other offences were committed by these people.   They married one wife, and they
held a festival on the day of the wedding.   All the relations
assembled, among whom were the principal people in the
country ; there was much drinking, and the parents took
the woman and delivered her to the chief, or to him who
was to be her husband.   The sons of this woman were those
who inherited the lordship or house.   The chiefs took many
other women without this ceremony, who lived with the
principal wife, and she in no way treated them ill or became
jealous of them, but ruled over them, and they obeyed her
as their mistress.   The sons of these other women were
looked upon as bastards, and inherited no share of their
father's property, like the sons of the principal wife ; but
those who inherited the house, looked upon the others and
maintained them as sons of the house.   These women had to

take care of each other on pain of death. The people had
certain chosen men called *Tecuria,* who were said to converse
with the devil, whom they called *Turia.* The *Tecuria* had a
very small hut with no door, and no covering overhead. The
chosen person went there at night, and talked with the
devil, who conversed in divers tones; and the chosen
person told the chief what he pleased afterwards, saying
that the devil had given him such and such answers. In
these provinces there were sorcerers and witches who did
much harm to children, and even to grown up people, at the
suggestion of the devil, who gave them his salves, with
which they anointed those whom they bewitched. These
salves were made from certain herbs. On inquiring in what
form the devil appeared, it was stated that he took the form
of a beautiful boy, in order that the people, being simple,
might not be terrified, and might believe him. They did
not see his hands, but on his feet he had three claws, like
those of a griffin. And in all the mischief that these witches
did, they were assisted by the devil, who entered the houses
with them. These and many other things are contained in
the information which I received from the witches themselves, who said that they anointed people with the salves
which were given to them by the enemy. It was affirmed
that, on a certain night, a witch was seen in a village with
many other women, and that, at the same hour, she was
seen at a farm where there were servants of her master,
a league and-a-half distant.[1]

Wishing to know whether these people had any notion of
God, I learnt that they knew of the flood of Noah, and they
said that he escaped in a canoe with his wife and sons; and
that the world had afterwards been peopled by them. They
believed that there was a God in heaven, whom they called
Chipiripa, and that he caused the rain, and sent down the
other things which fall from heaven. There is no report con-

[1] This statement is quoted by Herrera, Dec. ii, lib. i, cap. 3.

cerning the origin of these people, nor can they give any, except that they are natives of the country. There was a principal woman of this land who said that there was a belief among the chiefs (for the common people do not talk of these things), that there is a beautiful woman with a child in heaven; but the story goes no further.

The principal wives of the chiefs, whose sons inherit the lordships, have the title of *Hespode*, besides their own name, as who should say countess or marchioness. It was the custom in the land that, when a chief died, the wives whom it was supposed he loved best, should voluntarily be buried with their husband, and, if the chief had pointed them out, this was done whether they liked it or not. These were girls who had not been legitimate wives. When a chief died, he was adorned with gold, and wrapped in the richest cloths. His heir, who had become the chief, with all the family of his father, and the principal people of the land, then assembled and hung up the chief's body by cords, placing many pans of charcoal round it. The body was melted by the heat of the fire, and two vases were placed underneath, to catch the grease. When it was quite dried, it was hung up in the chief's palace. All the time that the body was being dried, ten of the principal men remained in the palace, where it was, day and night, seated round it, somewhat apart, dressed in black mantles which covered them from head to foot, and concealed the face and the whole body. No other person entered the place where they watched with the dead. These watchers had a drum which gave out a deep sound, and one of them struck blows on it from time to time as a sign of mourning. When he who played on the drum ceased his blows, he commenced a response in the same tone, and all the others with him, and then continued doing this for a long time with much mourning, with their faces covered, as I have already mentioned. Having finished these responses at two hours after midnight, while all the people in the house were watching, they gave so great a shout and howl that I, and those who were with me, jumped out of bed and seized our arms, not being able to imagine what was the matter. After a short space a deep silence followed, and the mourners then began to laugh and drink; except the twelve watchers who never quitted the dead night or day. When they were obliged to go out for a moment, their faces and bodies were entirely covered. I was present, as I have said, at the obsequies of a chief called Pocorosa, in the province of Cueva, and, wishing to know why they did these things, I was told that it was the custom, and that, in those hours when they shouted, they were repeating the history of the chief. On the anniversary of the day that he died, in the following year, they celebrate a festival in his honour, bringing all the food he used to eat, and the arms with which he fought, and models of the canoes in which he navigated, made with small sticks, into the presence of the body. They then take the body into a court which has been cleaned out, and burn it to ashes, saying that the smoke goes to the place where the dead man's soul is.[1] On asking them where that was, they replied that they only knew that it was in heaven, and that the smoke went there. And they continue to celebrate these anniversaries for the dead, if he was a person who could afford it, for much is spent on these occasions in eating and drinking. They have no ceremony or worship in this land, but they live by the laws of nature, keeping the laws not to kill, not to steal, and not to take another's wife. They know not what evidence is, but they hold it to be a very evil thing to lie. They also refrain from taking their father's principal wives, their sisters, or daughters for wives, because they hold it to be wrong.

In these provinces the weapons of the Indians are darts

---

[1] Herrera quotes this account of the obsequies of the cacique Pocorosa, from Andagoya. Dec. ii, lib. i, cap. 3.

and *macanas* (clubs).   The people were warlike, for their
chiefs. were continually at war with each other respecting
boundaries.   There are quantities of deer, and of swine
which are different from those of Spain, and they go in
large herds.   They have no tails, and they do not grunt,
even when they are killed.   They have something re-
sembling a navel on their backs.[1]

The chiefs had grounds, where they went to hunt in
summer.   They lighted fires to windward, and, as the
grass is high, the fires were great.   The Indians were
placed· in readiness to leeward, and as the stags fled half
blinded with the smoke, the fire obliged them to go
where the Indians waited with their darts pointed with
stones.   Few of the animals that fled from the fire,
escaped the darts.   They have no other game in these
provinces excepting birds, of which there are two kinds

---

[1] These are the peccaries. They have no tail, and no external toe to
the hind feet. Upon the back they have a glandular opening, from
which issues a fetid excretion. This gland was mistaken by Andagoya
and many other old writers for a navel. (See *Cieza de Leon*, p. 37, and
Alonzo Enriquez, p. 89.) The peccary is more easily tamed than the
wild boar of Europe and Asia. Azara says that the flesh is good, but
that it is necessary to cut off the dorsal gland immediately after death,
or it will taint the whole body. The Indians, however, eat peccaries
without taking this precaution. The head of a peccary is shorter and
thicker than that of a common pig, and the body, neck, and legs shorter.
Their bristles are very stiff. There are two species, the common and the
white lipped peccary. The former go in large herds conducted by a male
leader, the latter in pairs or in small numbers. The best account of the
peccary is to be found in the work of Don Felix d'Azara.

Acosta speaks " of the little pigs of the Indies with that strange pecu-
liarity of having a navel on their backs. They are cruel," he says, "and
fearless, and they have tusks as sharp as razors, with which they deal out
awkward stabs and cuts. Those who hunt them take refuge in the trees,
and the pigs bite the trunks with rage, when they cannot get at the men,
who throw darts at them. They are very good eating, but it is necessary to cut out the navel on the back at once, or otherwise the whole
carcass will be tainted within a day." *Historia Natural de Indias*, lib. iv,
cap. 38. See also *Herrera*, dec. ii, lib. ii, cap. 4.

c

uf turkeys,[1] pheasants,[2] doves, and many other sorts. There
are lions and tigers,[3] which do harm to the people, so that,
on their account, the houses were built very close to each
other, and were secured at night.   There is plenty of good
fish in the rivers.   The trees are green all the year round,
but very few of them bear fruit, yet on what fruit there is,
the people subsist.   There are three or four kinds of cats.
There are also certain vermin, smaller than foxes, which get
into the houses and eat the fowls.   On one side of their
bodies they carry a bag into which they put their young,
and take them about in this way constantly while they are
small.   Even when these creatures run or jump the young
cannot fall out, nor are they visible until the mothers are
killed, and the bag is opened.[4]

Vasco Nuñez, being in Darien after he had undergone
his *residencia*, sent one Francisco Garavita to the island
of Cuba, without the knowledge of Pedrarias.   Garavita returned with a ship and some men to the port of Darien, which
is a league and a half from the town.   Without disembark-
ing his men, he made known to Vasco Nuñez that he had
arrived.   This came to the knowledge of Pedrarias, and he
discovered that the vessel came to take Vasco Nuñez to the
South Sea, where he intended to form a settlement. So Pedrarias seized Vasco Nuñez, and made a cage in his own house,
into which he put him, and being there, he made an agreement with him, and gave him his daughter in marriage,
who was then in Spain.[5]   Having thus received Vasco
Nuñez as his son-in-law, Pedrarias sent him to the province
of Acla to form a settlement, being that which is now called

---

[1] Turkeys are natives of Mexico, and do not come further south than
Guatemala.   The bird alluded to by Andagoya is probably a curassow.

[2] There are no pheasants in America.   Andagoya no doubt alludes to
the crax, or penelope of the South American forests.

[3] Pumas and jaguars.

[4] Opossums.

[5] This was arranged through the intervention of Juan de Quevedo,

Acla. Thence Vasco Nuñez sent people to the Rio de la Balsa, and made two ships, that he might embark on the South Sea, and discover what there might be in it.[1]

Vasco Nuñez came to that river, near a populous district which had no chief, for the heads of families were the chiefs among that people; and all lived in friendship with each other. This province borders on that of Cueva, and the people are the same. It is wooded and flat, and fertile in yielding crops for bread. In this river we made two ships; and we brought many Indians to Acla, to carry the materials for the ships, and the food for the carpenters and other workmen.[2] We conveyed these ships down to the sea with great labour, for we met with many torrents forming hollows, which we had to cross. Having got down to the gulf of San Miguel, there was a high tide, and, as the carpenters did not know the wood, it proved to be such that all the planks were eaten through, and honeycombed.[3] Thus there was much trouble before we could pass in the ships to the islands of Pearls, where they came to pieces, and we made others of good timber, which were larger and better.

Vasco Nuñez was to be absent on this expedition for a year and a half, at the end of which time he was to send an account of what he had done to the governor.

the bishop of Darien, who had become a firm friend of Vasco Nuñez. The betrothal was a mere measure of expediency on the part of Vasco Nuñez, who was deeply attached to an Indian girl, the daughter of the cacique Careta.

[1] The scheme of Vasco Nuñez was to cut and fashion the frames of his vessels at Acla, then to carry the pieces over the forest covered hills, put them together on the banks of the Rio de la Balsa, and so descend into the South Sea, and commence his grand career of discovery. Certainly a bold and difficult undertaking, worthy of the man. Andagoya served in this, the last expedition of the intrepid Vasco Nuñez.

[2] As many as five hundred Indians are said to have perished in carrying the timber, ropes, and iron across the terrible *sierra*, with its dense forests and rapid torrents. Both Spaniards and Indians suffered fearfully from want of provisions.

[3] Fresh timber, we are told by Herrera, had to be hewn on the banks

At this time the King heard of the differences in the government, arising from the officers having votes, and he ordered that Pedrarias should govern alone. As Vasco Nuñez had never paid much respect to the officials, nor sent them any of the Indians that he had captured, as the other captains did, they bore him no good will, and they said to the governor that he had rebelled. They persuaded the governor to go to Acla, that he might get news of Vasco Nuñez and send for him, and the officials accompanied the governor. At this time Vasco Nuñez, having built the ships, came to the gulf of San Miguel, and landed in a populous district called Pequeo, where he remained for two months, seizing Indians and sending them to Acla for more cordage or pitch, which were required for the ships. Here we received news that Lope de Sosa had been appointed in Castile to come out to this land as governor. So Vasco Nuñez assembled certain of his friends who were honourable men, and it was arranged that one Valderrabano should go with a small force in company with the Indians, and that he should secretly send a man to the neighbourhood of Acla, who should go at night to the house of Vasco Nuñez and find out the news about the new governor.[1] If it was true all the people were to return, that the new governor might not break up the expedition, and we were to have gone to settle at Chepabar, which is six leagues nearer Acla than

of the river; but when it was placed on the stocks, the tide came up so high as to carry away part of it, and bury the rest in the mud. The workmen had to save themselves by climbing up the trees.

[1] The plan was that one Francisco Garavita should go back to Acla, and send in a man named Luis Botello to learn the news. If Lope de Sosa had arrived, Vasco Nuñez intended to have sailed away on his discovery, but if Pedrarias was still in power, then the emissaries were to have applied for further supplies of pitch and iron. This resolution was made by Vasco Nuñez in a conversation with Valderrabano, a notary, one evening in a hut. It so happened that it came on to rain, and a sentry, sheltering himself under the eaves, overheard just so much as to make him think that Vasco Nuñez intended to sail away on the discovery on his own account, and make himself independent of Pedrarias.

Panama.   But the man was seized for having come in
at night like a spy, and because the governor had ordered
that any one who arrived was to be sent to Darien.   Soon
afterwards the governor, with the officials, arrived at Acla ;
and when Valderrabano came in, he sent his letters to
the governor.   The officials began to accuse Vasco Nuñez,
and advised that he should be sent for and made prisoner ;
so the governor wrote him a letter, ordering him to come
and disprove the things of which he was accused.[1]   Vasco
Nuñez presently arrived, and was put into a house at Acla
as his prison, with guards over him.[2]   Pedrarias, considering
him as his son-in-law, would not act in the matter, but
entrusted the case to the licentiate Espinosa, who was
Alcalde Mayor.   This official drew up the process, and
sentenced Vasco Nuñez, Valderrabano, Botello who was the
man that had been sent into Acla at night, and Arguello,

[1] Francisco Garavita, the former friend of Vasco Nuñez, appears to
have poisoned the mind of Pedrarias against his intended son-in-law, by
telling that irritable old man that there was an intention to throw off his
authority, and to sail away with the vessels on independent discovery.
Las Casas says that Garavita's motive for this treason to his friend was
that both loved the beautiful daughter of the cacique Careta.   This
induced the truculent and suspicious old governor to come to Acla with
his officials, and there he heard the story of the eaves-dropping sentry.
He then wrote a letter to Vasco Nuñez, requesting him to return to
Acla, to confer with him on business, intending to get him into his
power, and find some excuse for putting him out of the way.

[2] A Venetian astrologer, named Codro, had once told Vasco Nuñez
that in the year in which he should see a certain star in a certain part of
the heavens, he would run great risk of his life.   One evening, just before
he received the summons from Pedrarias, he saw the fatal star in the
quarter indicated by the astrologer, and laughed at his prediction, for
the great discoverer deemed himself to be on the high road to fortune,
with four ships and three hundred men ready to navigate the South Sea.
Vasco Nuñez, quite unsuspicious of any treachery, set out at once to obey
the summons of Pedrarias, and was arrested on the road by his old com-
panion in arms—Francisco Pizarro.   The great discoverer exclaimed,
" What is this, Francisco ? You were not wont to come out in this
fashion to receive me."   He was put into confinement, and the licentiate

who was the friend of Vasco Nuñez, and had sent him certain letters,[1] to have their heads cut off.[2]

This sentence having been executed, Pedrarias set out for the islands of Pearls with all the troops that were at Acla. The ships were there, with the people who had remained in the South Sea. Thence he went in the ships to Panama, where he founded the present city,[3] the rest of the people going round by land with the licentiate Espinosa. The governor divided the land amongst the four hundred citizens who then settled in Panama, leaving a certain portion

Espinosa was ordered to proceed against him, using the evidence of Garavita and the sentry.

[1] Hernando de Arguello was the last victim. His crime was that he had written to warn Vasco Nuñez of his danger, and his letter was intercepted. The sun had set before his turn came, and the people entreated Pedrarias to spare him, but the hateful old man exclaimed: " I would sooner die myself than spare one of them." He was executed in the dark.

[2] The death of Vasco Nuñez was one of the greatest calamities that could have happened to South America at that time. He had collected his little fleet in the bay of San Miguel, and was about to sail away into the unknown ocean which he had discovered. He would thus have become the discoverer of the great empire of the Yncas, and the conquest of Peru would have formed a very different story from that which is now interwoven with the ill-omened name of Pizarro. For Vasco Nuñez was one of those men who are born to govern their fellows. He had the true genius of a statesman and a warrior, was as humane and judicious as he was firm of purpose and indomitable of will. And this great man was destined to fall through the mean jealousy of a miserable old dotard, whom chance had kicked into power. His execution took place in 1517. He was in his forty-second year.

Oviedo says that Pedrarias witnessed the judicial murder of Vasco Nuñez from between the reeds of a wall which was close to the scaffold. " For this inhuman act," says Herrera, " Pedrarias was never called to account, but on the contrary was continued in the government."

[3] Herrera says that Panama was much disliked by the settlers, on account of its unhealthy situation, and that 40,000 men were computed to have died there of disease within the first twenty-eight years after the founding of the city. Tello de Guzman had landed at Panama (*a place abounding in fish* in the Indian language) in 1515, and Pedrarias founded the city in 1519. It received its privileges from Charles V in 1521.

of the province of Cueva for the citizens of Acla. But as the captains, who had made many incursions into the country from Darien, had carried off great numbers of Indians, and as the land was of small extent from one sea to the other, there were very few Indians at the time that the land was divided, and the governor could give only ninety Indians in *repartimiento*, or fifty or forty. And as each cacique had to give nearly all his Indians, who were required to till the ground and build houses, and as those that remained were taken off to the mines, where they died, in a short time neither chiefs nor Indians were to be found in all the land.[1]

Panama was founded in the year 1519, on the day of Nuestra Señora de Agosto, and at the end of that year a captain named Diego Alvites founded Nombre de Dios, by order of Pedrarias.[2] In Nombre de Dios there was a certain race of people called *Chuchures*, with a language different from that of the other Indians. They came to settle in this place in canoes from Honduras, and as the country was unhealthy their numbers decreased, and there were few of them. Of these few none survived the treatment they received after Nombre de Dios was founded.

Having founded Panama in this year, the governor sent the licentiate Espinosa in command of the ships, with as many men as they would hold, to the westward.[3] The licentiate arrived at the province of Burica, on the coast of Nicaragua, some hundred leagues from Panama. Thence

---

[1] This hideous picture of the devastation caused by the Spaniards, within a few years after their first arrival, is but too true.

[2] The town of Nombre de Dios was abandoned in the reign of Philip II, on account of its extreme unhealthiness, and Porto Bello became the chief Atlantic port of the isthmus. In later times Porto Bello was abandoned for Chagres, and now Colon or Aspinwall is the Atlantic terminus of the Panama railway.

[3] These were the vessels constructed with such immense toil and difficulty by Vasco Nuñez.

he turned to come back by land, sending a ship to explore
a gulf which they called San Lucar, in Nicaragua. The
ship brought back news respecting that land; and the
Licentiate, returning by land to Panama from the province
of Burica, came, with as many men as he could spare, to the
province of Huista. Here he remained for some time,
loading the ships with maize, and sending it to Panama,
because there was great scarcity and little land that was
inhabited.

The people of this province and of that of Burica, were
almost exactly the same in the fashion of their clothes, and
in their customs. The women wore a truss round their
loins, as their clothing; and the men were naked. The
country is fertile, with plentiful supplies of fish, and a great
quantity of swine, which were caught with large nets of
stuff like hemp, called by the Indians *nequen*, the meshes
being a finger in breadth. These nets were fastened at the
entrance of a wood where there was a herd of swine, who
came against the nets and were unable to get through the
meshes. Then the people called out, the nets fell over the
swine, and they were killed with lances, so that none
escaped, of those that fell into the nets.[1]

Leaving this province on our way to Panama by land, we
arrived at a mountainous district, with a cold climate, where
we found some forests of very beautiful oaks covered with
acorns. There were three or four chiefs in this province,
and their villages were well fortified with pallisades made of
very strong thorny plants, intertwined, and forming a thick
wall. Throughout these districts the Indians were seized
and bound. From Burica to this province, which is called
Tobreytrota, nearly every chief has a different language
from the others. From this hilly country we turned to
descend towards the sea, and came to the province of Nata,

[1] This account of the manner of hunting peccaries is quoted by
Herrera. Dec. ii, lib. i, cap. 3.

where the town was founded which is now called Nata.[1] At
first it received the name of Santiago, and it is 30 leagues
from Panama. This was a very populous province, inhabited by a very good, hard working people. The chief
of this land continually led his men of war against his
neighbours. His chief enemy was a lord named Escoria,
who had his villages on the banks of a great river, eight
leagues from Meta. Here he had very large deposits of
salt, which are made naturally by the water which flows into
the sea, in certain lakes formed by the increase of fresh
water, where it crystallises in the summer. Eight leagues
further on, in the direction of Panama, there was another
chief called Chiru, whose people have a different language,
although their appearance, dress, and way of living is the
same as that of their neighbours. Seven leagues from Chiru,
towards Panama, is the province of Chame, which is the
point to which the language of Coiba extends.

In the year 1516, a captain named Gonzalo de Badajos set
out with a small force which was placed under his command
by Pedrarias, and, going by sea, disembarked at Nombre
de Dios.[2] Thence he went along the skirts of the mountains, through the territory of certain chiefs, until he came
out at Chiru, which we shall describe further on. From
Chiru he went to the province of Nata. The Indians had

[1] William Funnel thus describes Nata in 1703. " The town of Nata
is a large and well compacted town, situated upon the banks of a river
of the same name. It has great trade with Panama, selling them provisions, as cows, hogs, fowls, and maize. From Nata the coast stretches
in mountains and hills, and the water is so shoal that there is scarcely
any coming in for a ship ; but if there were, here is never a port. Along
this coast ships ought to keep two or three leagues off shore, or else they
will meet with broken ground and sunk rocks ; but the coast has many
fresh water rivers, full of several sorts of very good fish." *Collection of
Voyages* (London, 1729), iv, p. 95.

[2] Herrera says he had a force of 130 men, and that his orders were to
conquer all the country between Nombre de Dios and the South Sea.
This expedition took place during the lifetime of Vasco Nuñez.

never seen Spaniards, and held such people to have fallen
from the skies, and they would not attack them until they
knew whether they would die. Thus the Spaniards went
from Nata and Escoria, without having recourse to war,
and came to the province of Paris, which is twelve leagues
from Nata to the westward; for nearly all this land, as far
as Nicaragua, trends to the westward. The chief of Paris,
with his people, concealed himself from the Spaniards, who
had brought two principal men from Nata as guides and
interpreters. These men, seeing that no natives appeared,
proposed to go in search of them, and get speech with the
chief. They started one morning, and came back in the
afternoon with a boy, who said that the chief was in a village three or four leagues off, with all his household and
wives. They were sent with the boy to ask him to come, as
the strangers only desired peace and friendship. The chief,
whose name was Quitatara, sent back eleven *castellanos* of
good gold, saying that his women sent them, and asking
the Spaniards to leave his country, as he did not wish to
see them. The captain, moved to avarice at the sight of
this gold, sent back to summon him, saying that if he did
not come, he would go in search of him. The chief had
spies to watch when the Christians should set out from the
camp. When the captain took one road and the Indians
another, the chief fell upon those who remained in the
camp with such fury that the Spaniards were defeated, and
fled to a height, with the loss of some killed and others
wounded. The flight was so hurried that the Indians took
the hut where there were fifty and more thousand *pesos* of
gold, which up to that time had been collected. It was set
on fire before all the gold could be taken out, and, the fire
reaching it, a bag containing eight *pesos* was burnt, for which
reason they left it there. The captain, as he was travelling
by land in the morning, met the Indians coming in warlike array, towards the place where the Christians re-

mained; and on inquiring for the chief, they said that he
was at the Christian camp. On hearing this, the captain
returned with great speed, and when he arrived, he found
his people all wounded and maltreated.[1] As his own party
was fresh, he defeated the Indians, and, not wishing to
wait for a battle on the following day, he embarked on a
river that flowed near the village, in certain canoes, and
went out to sea; proceeding to Nata with the chief of that
place, who had come with him. Having heard the news of
the defeat of the Christians, the Indians prepared for war;
and the Christians, entering Nata without precaution, because they had left the place at peace, were met by the
Indians, who came out to fight them with great fury. They
fought almost all day, without either one side or the other
being defeated. Not wishing to wait another day, the
Christians went down to the place where they had left the
canoes, during the night, and went in them to the province
of Comogre, which is adjoining to Acla.

In the same year, six months after this captain departed,
Pedrarias left Darien with all the troops he had with him,
and went over to the other coast of Carthagena, below
Cenu, to obtain tidings of a captain named Becerra, who
had set out from Darien with one hundred and seventy
men, and had not been heard of since. Marching inland
we came to a very high hill, where there was a small village.
The Indians defended themselves with their arrows, and
wounded the Spaniards, but at last the heights were gained,
and it was gathered from the few people who were captured,
that Becerra and all his men had been killed by Indians,
while crossing a river. After receiving this news the
governor returned to the coast, embarked, and went to the

---

[1] Badajoz took great care in dressing the wounds of his men. He
sewed them up with pack thread, used the grease of the Indians who had
been killed instead of oil, and bound them with bandages made of their
own shirts. Thus many recovered. *Herrera.*

provinco of Aola, to the place where the town now stands.
He was there taken ill, so he returned to Darien, and sent
the licentiate Gaspar de Espinosa, with all the troops he
could collect, in a westerly direction.

The first inhabited district we came to was that of Comogre, and, being in Chiman (two leagues beyond Comogre)
we heard that Badajoz was passing along the high road, at
a distance of about a league from the place where we had
pitched our camp. On sending for tidings from him, we
learnt that he had been defeated in Paris, and had been
flying through all the districts on the road. He gave us a
guide to show us the way by which he had come, and thus
we went from Chiman to the province of Pocorosa, and
thence a journey of two leagues in a westerly direction
brought us to Pararaca, where the district of Coiba commences. Thence four leagues in the same direction brought
us to Tubanama, eight leagues more to Chepo, six more to
Chepobar, two further on to Pacora, four more to Panama,
four more to Periquete, four more to Tabore, and four more to
Chame, which is the boundary of the language and province
of Coiba.

We found all these provinces well peopled, and we passed
through them without having recourse to war, for we had
with us two horses, there then not being more in the land,
and one hundred and fifty men.[1] From Chame to the province

---

[1] Herrera says that Espinosa met with opposition in Comogre and
Pocorosa. He tried the prisoners, being a lawyer, hanging some, and
cutting off the noses or hands of others, according to their alleged crimes.
These civilians were often more cruel than the rudest soldiers. Well
might Vasco Nuñez wish to be rid of all lawyers. In a letter to the
king he says: "Most puissant lord, I desire to ask a favour of your
Highness, and it is that your Highness will command that no bachelor of
laws, nor of anything else unless it be of medicine, shall come to this
part of the Indies on pain of heavy punishment, which your Highness
shall order to be inflicted; for no bachelor of laws has ever come here
who is not a devil, and who does not lead the life of a devil. And not
only are they themselves evil, but they give rise to a thousand quarrels.

of Chiru is eight leagues of uninhabited country in the same direction; and this Chiru is inhabited by a well disposed people, with a language of their own. From this province to that of Nata there are four leagues of uninhabited country. All these districts are fertile and level,—a very fine land abounding in supplies of maize, *aji*, melons different from those here, grapes, and *yucas*; with excellent fishing in the rivers and in the sea, and deer fit for the chace. The districts of Coiba and Cueva are the same in these respects.

We wintered in Nata, and during the period of our sojourn we collected large supplies of maize, and of all things else that the district yielded. The chief retired to a small hill in the centre of his territory with the greater part of his people, and, as we left them without the food they had gathered for the year, they suffered much from hunger, insomuch that many came down to our camp, that we might take them, and give them food. Thus a great number were captured. After the winter, we set out in the same direction, and came to the province of Escoria, six leagues from Nata. Here we captured the chief, and went on to the province of Paris, passing the place where the Indians had defeated the Christians. We then approached another village where the chief was, who came out to us to give us battle on a plain, and this battle was fought with great ferocity, and lasted from nine in the morning until an hour before sunset, when several were wounded. It pleased God that the Indians should be broken and defeated.

We remained there that night, and next day, following the path to the village where the chief was, we came to it, and found that it had been entirely destroyed. Passing

This order would be greatly to the advantage of your Highness's service." Gaspar de Espinosa afterwards took an important part in the discovery of Peru, having advanced money to Pizarro for his expedition. He fell ill and died at Cuzco, while engaged in negotiating between Pizarro and Almagro.

onwards for three leagues we reached the territory of
a chief, a vassal of Paris, named Ubsagano, where we found
a very great quantity of maize crops ripe for harvest, which
we reaped.   Here we formed our camp, intending to make
war upon Paris from this place, until he should give us the
gold that he had taken from Gonzalo de Badajoz.   We
pressed him so hard that, not wishing to come out to fight
again, he consulted with one and the other of his vassals,
and determined to give us the gold in order that we might
desist.   But, not wishing us to believe that he did so
because he was afraid, he arranged that two Indians should
let themselves be captured by us, and tell us where the gold
was from fear.   The gold was on a hill apart from the
village that had been burnt, in a little hut which had been
built for it.   These Indians showed us the way, and thus
the gold was recovered, without anything being lost.

This Cutatura, the chief of Paris, was a brave man, and
conquered the provinces of Suema, Chicacotra, Sangana,
and Guarage in war.   He was always at war with the
people of Escoria ; and those of Escoria came to this same
land of Paris and made war during eight days, and no day
passed without a battle being fought.   In Escoria there was
a race of Indians, much larger and more polished than the
others, among whom there were knights who were held
to be very valiant.   Their breasts and arms were worked
over with certain chains in links and curves.   Very few
of these survived the battles in Paris; but I saw some,
by the side of whom the other Indians looked like dwarfs.
They were very handsome and well made.   As they were
waging war in the land of another, and as the vassal chiefs
of Paris could retire each day to refresh themselves, the
latter maintained the war with more ease.   Finally, they
threw away their arms, and closed in an embrace, biting each
other.   As those of Escoria were bigger and stronger than
those of Paris, they worsted them ; so that, for want of

arms, those of Paris fled, and the number that died on the road to their homes was such, that trenches were made, into which the dead were put. We saw these, and, where the battle took place, we found a great street entirely paved with the heads of the dead, and at the end of it a tower of heads which was such that a man on horseback could nòt see over it.

The languages of Escoria and Nata are different, and each chief has a different language, so that they require interpreters. In this land of Paris there are great quantities of deer and *dantas* ;[1] but the Indians of war never eat meat, except fish and iguanas, though the Indians, who are labourers, do eat flesh. In all these districts the people wear the same dress as those of Coiba, except that in Paris their mantles are dyed with very bright colours. In food and everything else they follow the habits of those of Cueva and Coiba. They have no more notion of the things appertaining to God than the others, nor have they different rites and ceremonies.

From this expedition we returned to Darien with a great number of persons, so that, in order to make a day's journey of three or four leagues, we had to cut two roads for the people to pass along. These people, with all the others who went to Darien, ended their days there. It was seen that in Darien there were no Indians, unless they were brought from other distant provinces ; and as they all died there, the settlement was removed to Acla, and thus Darien was abandoned.

In the year 1517 Gil Gonzalez de Avila[2] arrived at Darien with a certain capitulation which he had made with His Majesty, accompanied by carpenters and labourers to build

---

[1] Tapirs.

[2] He had been accountant of Hispaniola, and was formerly in the household of the bishop of Burgos, who appointed him to the command of this expedition to discover and conquer Nicaragua.

ships, and all the necessary fittings for them, to be put together in the Rio de la Balsa, and their futtock-timbers were
brought ready shaped from Spain. They disembarked at
Acla, and Gil Gonzalez went to Darien, to secure the support of the governor, for his enterprise. The ships, having
been built in the Rio de la Balsa, were sent down to
the sea, passed the island of Pearls, and, Panama having
been peopled in 1519, the flotilla was brought there.[1] This
Gil Gonzalez had to discover a certain number of leagues to
the westward, concerning which the capitulation had been
made; and thus he coasted along and arrived at the gulf of
San Lucar, which had already been discovered by Pedrarias.
It is at the commencement of the land of Nicaragua. Having
passed the place where Leon and Granada now stand, he disembarked, and came to a village where he found one hundred
thousand *pesos de oro*.[2] As soon as his arrival was known
in the land, a large force of warlike Indians came against
him, and obliged him to fall back and embark again, as he
had not sufficient force to resist them.[3] He returned to
Panama with the gold,[4] and went thence to Spain; but
returned to San Domingo, and equipped an expedition
to settle in Nicaragua, going by way of Honduras.

At this time Pedrarias sent one Francisco Hernandez de
Cordova in command of a force, to subdue and settle
Nicaragua; and he entered that land, subduing and conquering, and fighting in many skirmishes and battles. He
founded the cities of Leon and Granada, and built fortresses
in them, for defence. This land was very populous and
fertile, yielding supplies of maize, and many fowls of the

[1] Herrera says that the ships were built in the island of Terequeri, in
the bay of San Miguel; and the expedition sailed on January 21st, 1522.
Gil Gonzalez took with him Andres Niño as his pilot, and many Indians.

[2] Here he met with a powerful chief named Nicaragua.

[3] He discovered the whole coast of Nicaragua, as far as the gulf of
Fonseca, which he called after his patron the bishop of Burgos.

[4] In June 1523.

country, and certain small dogs which they also eat, and many deer and fish. It is a very salubrious land. The Indians were very civilised in their way of life, like those of Mexico, for they were a people who had come from that country, and they had nearly the same language.[1] These people went about well dressed in the Indian fashion; the women with their mantles like those of Coiba, and another description of covering which, descending from the head, covered the bosom and half the arms. The men covered their loins with very long cloths made of cotton, which they passed in many folds from the hips to the thighs. In the villages they wore their mantles like cloaks under the arms. They had a great quantity of cotton cloth, and they held their markets in the open squares, where they traded. The land was poor in gold, and they traded with cacao, as in New Spain. They had many beautiful women. Their parents had a custom, when they were maidens old enough to marry, of sending them to work for their marriages, and thus they went through the land working publicly, and as soon as they had wherewithal to furnish a house, they returned to their parents and were married. The husbands were so much under subjection that if they made their wives angry, they were turned out of doors, and the wives even raised their hands against them. The husband would go to the neighbours and beg them to ask his wife to let him come back, and not be angry with him. The wives made their husbands attend on them, and do everything like servant lads.[2] They had another custom, which was that when one of them was married, a man whom they held as a pope, and who lived in a temple, had to sleep

[1] Five languages were spoken in Nicaragua. The *Charibizi*, the *Cholotecan* (being the most ancient), the *Choutal*, the *Orotinan*, and Mexican. *Herrera*.

[2] Herrera also says that the men swept the houses and performed other menial services, and that in some places they even spun, having their arms naked and painted.

D

with the bride on the previous night. In this temple there
was a statue of gold, to which they sacrificed through the
instrumentality of him who was there as priest, and their
sacrifice was that, in the presence of the statue, they tore
out the hearts of men and women who were sacrificed, and
anointed the statue with them. They also cut out the
tongues with certain stones like razors, and anointed the
statue with them.[1] Likewise they offered up much game
and fish, and other eatables, and of these the priest, who
resided there, did eat. The Indians made a sort of confes-
sion of certain sins which appeared to them to be heinous,
and they thought that, by confessing them to this priest,
they were freed from them.

This is a land of abundance of good fruit, and of honey
and wax, wherewith all the neighbouring countries are supplied. The bees are very numerous, some of them yellow,
and these do not sting. They deposit the honey under the
ground. There are many wolves in this land, which live
upon the deer. They make wine from a kind of cherry,
which is as strong as the wine of Spain, although the
strength soon passes away. In all the countries I have
mentioned the whole happiness of the people consists in
drinking the wine they make from maize, which is like
beer, and on this they get as drunk as if it was the wine of
Spain, and all the festivals they hold, are for the purpose of
drinking.

In this province there is a volcano from which smoke
constantly issues, and at night it may be seen for three
leagues round. At night it looks like flame, and in the day
time like smoke.[2] The mouth is round like that of a well,

[1] The priest went thrice round the victim, singing a doleful hymn,
then tore out his heart, and cut up the body. The priest ate the heart,
the cacique received the hands and feet, the man who had captured the
victim got the thighs, the trumpeter had the bowels, and the rest was
given to the people. *Herrera.*

[2] This is a burning mountain called Massaya, about three leagues from
Granada.

and half way down there is a ledge round the mouth; as when they make a well, the upper half is wider, and the lower half, being faced with masonry, is narrower, and ends upwards in a sort of ledge. At times the fire comes out with great fury, and sends forth many stones, that look like great fiery pieces of iron. I have seen this, and it seems that the fire has worked on them, and left them as cinders. They destroy the herbage for half a league round; and the Indians, to appease the fire so that it may not come and destroy them, bring a virgin there, at certain times of the year, to offer her up, and they throw her in. They are then joyful, for they believe that they are saved. In this sacrifice, and in those to the statue, many people die every year. A friar, they say, entered as far as the ledge half way down the mouth, and thence he looked down and saw a certain thing like metal, of the colour of fire, and he let down a link of an iron chain by a rope, but when he drew it up he found nothing.[1] I do not think it can be gold, because gold is cold, and if extreme force was not used, very little could be broken off. I believe that the fire contains what there is in it, and does not receive anything from any other source. This land is poor in gold. No mines have been found, except seventy leagues from Leon; and by taking the people from a warm and level country to dig out gold at such a distance and in high mountains, a very large part of the population has disappeared; and afterwards, there being no one to cultivate the land, the Spaniards began to make slaves, and to reward the chiefs who brought slaves to them. They were taken in great numbers to be sold at

[1] Fray Blas de Ymesta, and two other Spaniards, were let down into the first mouth in two baskets, with an iron bucket and a long chain, to draw up some of the fiery matter, which they believed to be gold. The chain went down for 150 fathoms, and as soon as it came to the fire, the bucket and some links of the chain melted. The gold seekers remained there that night, without wanting fire or candle, and came out again next morning in their baskets, very much frightened. *Herrera.*

Panama and in Peru, and these are the reasons why this country is now so much depopulated. The inhabitants have a manufactory, where they make cordage of a sort of *nequen*,[1] which is like carded flax; the cord is beautiful, and stronger than that of Spain, and their cotton canvas is excellent. Pitch and timber for ship building do not abound more in Biscay. In this province there are two lakes of sweet water, one of which drains itself into the North Sea, and the other is more than forty leagues long.[2] In them there are great fisheries.

Francisco Hernandez, who settled this land, finding himself powerful in the number of his followers, and being ill off in all things else, meditated a project to rise and throw off obedience to Pedrarias, or any one he might send. With this view, he assembled the principal people of the two settlements to induce them to write to his Majesty, praying that he might be appointed their governor. But the captains Francisco Campanon[3] and Soto, not only refused their assent, but condemned the proceedings. Fearing these captains and their followers (for there were ten or twelve who took counsel to resist his acts), he seized upon Soto, and put him into the fortress at Granada. Francisco Campanon, however, with nine of his friends, marched to Granada, and took Soto out of prison. The whole party then took the field, well armed and mounted. Francisco Hernandez, as soon as he knew this, came to Granada with sixty men, and found his opponents in the field; but he would not attack them, because he knew they would try to kill him before anyone else. The dissentients then took their way to Panama, and after many dangers and hard-

---

[1] A sort of *pita?*

[2] The lakes of Nicaragua and of Leon.

[3] Campanon had been one of the most active assistants of Vasco Nuñez when he conveyed the timber across the isthmus, for building his vessels. He established a resting place or halfway house on the top of the *sierra*.

ships, and having abandoned their horses because they could not pass that way, they arrived barefooted. They had passed the villages of the Indians at night, and taken provisions from them. Thus they had reached the province of Chiriqui, which is between Burica and Nisca, where there was a settlement which had been made by Captain Benito Hurtado, by order of Pedrarias, called the city of Fonseca. Here they were refreshed; and this captain gave them a canoe, in which they came as far as Nata. Having reported what had taken place to Pedrarias, he assembled ships and men to go to Nicaragua, captured Francisco Hernandez, and cut off his head.

After these ten Spaniards had passed through this city of Fonseca, the captain, with some followers, set out in the direction of Nicaragua, whence the others had come. Thus the settlement was abandoned; for those who remained, seeing that their comrades did not return, went after them to the gulf of San Lucar.

At this time the Marquis del Valle[1] passed near Nicaragua, when he went to Honduras; and Francisco Hernandez, desiring to revolt from Pedrarias, sent to invite the Marquis to come and receive the province from him. Gil Gonzalez, who set out from San Domingo in search of Nicaragua by way of Honduras, encountered, in a province called Manalca, the captain Soto, whom Francisco Hernandez had sent to that part. Soto resisted the passage of Gil Gonzalez through the district, and Gil Gonzalez stopped, and cunningly treated for peace. Soto, finding himself more powerful in numbers than his opponent, did not fear him; and though the one force was very close to the other, he did not set a guard on his camp. So, one night, Gil Gonzalez took him unawares, made him prisoner, and secured his arms. Of the troops who came out to resist, two men were killed with two arquebuses.

---

[1] Hernan Cortes, the conqueror of Mexico.

But Gil Gonzalos did not deem it prudent to keep these people in his company, so he released them, and seeing that there was no way to enter Nicaragua, he returned to Puerto de Cavallos, where was Cristoval de Olid, a captain of Cortes, and Casas, who was a captain sent also by Cortes in search of him. Gil Gonzalez being entirely in the power of Cristoval de Olid, one day, when he was at dinner, they stabbed him, and so he died.

Pedrarias being now in Nicaragua, he sent one Martin Estete, with some troops, to settle the province of Manalca ; but having founded a town, Don Pedro de Alvarado, of Guatemala, sent another captain, declaring that it was within his jurisdiction, and this other captain took the town from Martin Estete, who fled back to Pedrarias alone : so that other captain formed the town of San Miguel, which is now in the government of Guatemala.

We have already mentioned how Lope de Sosa came as governor of Tierra Firme, and, arriving in the port of Darien, died before he could land. Afterwards, Pedro de los Rios came as governor to this land ; and Pedrarias being in Nicaragua, the new governor arrived at Panama to take his *residencia*.[1] Pedro de los Rios then went to Nicaragua. At the time of his arrival, one Diego Lopez de Salcedo came from the province of Honduras, sent there as governor by the audience of San Domingo. He advanced into Nicaragua, and both reached Leon almost on the same day ; but Salcedo was so successful in getting help, although he brought no orders to that effect, that they received him as lieutenant of Pedrarias, and drove Pedro de los Rios out of the country, obliging him to return to Panama.

At that time the appointment of Pedrarias to the government of Nicaragua arrived, and he went there, where he

---

[1] Pedrarias had thus been governor of the isthmus from 1519 to 1526; but even now the old wretch was allowed to retain the government of Nicaragua, and he died at Leon in 1530.

died. After his death the Bishop Diego Alvarez Osorio
remained as governor, who died a short time after he had
assumed the government, leaving it in the hands of the
licentiate Castañeda, who had been alcalde mayor. This man
did such things that, on hearing that Rodrigo de Contreras,
the son-in-law of Pedrarias, was coming out as governor,
he went off to Peru with all his family. Rodrigo de Contreras governed until the present time; but he has lately
arrived at this court under arrest, and has been ordered to
return, that a *residencia* may be made. He did no good
thing worthy of record in that land, but persecuted honourable and married men.

In all these provinces, from Nicaragua to Darien, there
is not half an hour between day and night during the year;
and the summer lasts from the beginning of December
to the beginning of May. During this time the winds
blow from the north and north-east; it does not rain, or
become colder than in winter, and the people are healthy,
and it is a marvel if any are taken ill. The winter begins
in the early part of May, and lasts till the end of November;
and in September and August it rains more than in the
other months. It is hot, and there is thunder and lightning.
In this season people fall sick. During all the season the
wind blows from the S.S.E., until some shower causes it
to change. On this coast of Panama, as far as the gulf of
San Miguel, streams of fresh water enter the sea at every
quarter or half league.

In all the rivers which enter the sea, there are a great quantity of those serpents which we call lizards.[1] In the rivers
they do people harm; but on the land they are very torpid,
though they are ready to resist and defend themselves,
yet they cannot run fast. When I was in the province
of Guanate with thirty men, we surrounded one of these
serpents in a place where it could not swim, wishing to kill

[1] Alligators.

it for food. But it defended itself so fiercely that, though we stabbed it many times, we could not cut through its skin, and so by little and little, fighting all the way, it got down to the water.

Two years before we came to Paris, a great army of people arrived there, coming from the direction of Nicaragua; and they were so fierce that the natives came out to offer them all they wanted. They ate human flesh; and this filled the people of all the districts through which they passed with fear. In one province, bordering on Paris, called Tauraba, they encamped on a plain, to which they took the boys of the neighbouring villages, that they might eat them. Here a sore disease broke out amongst them, which made them raise their camp, and retire to the seashore. Cutatara, the lord of Paris, seeing them enfeebled by sickness and carelessly off their guard, from never having been resisted, fell upon them one morning, defeated them, and killed every one, so that none were saved. He took the spoil, among which was much gold, and became very rich.

In the year 1522, being Inspector-General of the Indians, I set out from Panama to visit the surrounding territory to the eastward; and after reaching the gulf of San Miguel, I went on to visit a province called Chochama, which is populous, and where the same language is spoken as in the districts of Cueva. Here I learnt how certain people came by sea in canoes to make war at every full moon; and the inhabitants of that province were so terrified at their approach, that they feared to go to sea to fish. These invaders came from a province called Birú, the name of which has been corrupted to Pirú. All the land in that direction was inhabited by a numerous and warlike people. To comply with the prayer of the people of Chochama that I would defend them, and in order to discover what there was further on, I sent to Panama for reinforcements.

Having received them, I took the chief of Chochama, with interpreters and guides, and marched for six or seven days, until I reached that province, which was called Birú.[1] I then ascended a great river for twenty leagues, and met with many chiefs and villages, and a very strong fortress at the junction of two rivers, with people guarding it. They placed their women and goods in safety, and defended it bravely. At last, having occupied a position above them, they were quickly defeated. They fought with large shields covering the whole body, and short spears; and as the space was confined, and at the first assault they mixed with the Spaniards armed with swords, they were easily routed. This is a very populous province, and extends as far as the place where now stands the city of San Juan, which is a distance of fifty leagues. After this defeat and the capture of the fort, the people did not dare to show themselves in arms again; but several chiefs came to treat for peace, and went through the acts and ceremonies which are required from those who become vassals of his Majesty. Afterwards others came; and seven important chiefs became friendly, among whom one of them was like a king over the others, and was recognised as such by them all.

In this province I received accounts both from the chiefs and from merchants and interpreters, concerning all the coast, and everything that has since been discovered, as far as Cuzco; especially with regard to the inhabitants of each province, for in their trading these people extend their wanderings over many lands. Taking new interpreters, and the principal chief of that land, who wished of his own accord to go with me, and show me other provinces of the coast which obeyed him, I descended to the sea. The ships followed the coast at some little distance from the land, while I went close in, in a canoe, discovering the ports.

[1] Birú was first visited by Gaspar de Morales, with Francisco Pizarro as his second in command. See page 9.

While thus employed, I fell into the water, and if it had not been for the chief, who took me in his arms and pulled me on to the canoe, I should have been drowned. I remained in this position until a ship came to succour me, and while they were helping the others, I remained for more than two hours wet through. What with the cold air and the quantity of water I had drunk, I was laid up next day, unable to turn.[1] Seeing that I could not now conduct this discovery along the coast in person, and that the expedition would thus come to an end, I resolved to return to Panama with the chief and interpreters who accompanied me, and report the knowledge I had acquired of all that land.[2]

This land had never been discovered either by Castilla del Oro, or by way of the gulf of San Miguel, and the province was called Pirú, because one of the letters of Birú has been corrupted, and so we call it Pirú, but in reality there is no country of that name.

As soon as Pedrarias heard the great news which I had brought, he was also told by the doctors that time alone could cure me, and in truth it was fully three years before I was able to ride on horseback. He therefore asked me to hand over the undertaking to Pizarro,[3]

[1] Montesinos says that the illness of Andagoya arose, not from a ducking, but from a fall from his horse, while showing off his horsemanship to the natives. But Andagoya himself must certainly have known best.

[2] Thus Andagoya was the first pioneer of the discovery of Peru.

[3] Francisco Pizarro was born at Truxillo, in Estremadura, in about the year 1471, the illegitimate child of a colonel of infantry. It is not known when he first crossed the Atlantic, but at 1510 he was at Hispaniola, and enlisted as a man at arms in the expedition of Alonzo de Ojeda to the gulf of Darien. Ojeda formed a settlement which he called San Sebastian de Uraba, and returned to Hispaniola for assistance, leaving the main body of his following under the command of Pizarro. The Spaniards suffered from famine and disease, and at last Pizarro embarked them all in two small vessels; but outside the harbour they met a ship which proved to be that of the Bachiller Enciso, Ojeda's partner, coming

Almagro,[1] and father Luque,[2] who were partners,[3] in order that so great a discovery might be followed up, and, he added, that they would repay me what I had expended. I replied that, so far as the expedition was concerned, I must give it up, but that I did not wish to be paid, because if they paid me my expenses they would not have sufficient to commence the business, for at that time they had not more than sixty dollars.

Accordingly, these three, and Pedrarias, which made four, formed a company, each partner taking a fourth share.[4] Guided by the narrative and the interpreters given them by me, they set out on the expedition with a ship and two canoes. Pizarro, suspicious of me, took a direction different to that which I have pointed out, and went to the province

with succour. Pizarro then sunk into a secondary position, and served under Vasco Nuñez de Balboa, who shortly afterwards deposed Enciso, and founded the colony of Darien. He accompanied Vasco Nuñez when he discovered the South Sea, was second in command under Gaspar de Morales in his ruthless expedition, and was the man who arrested Vasco Nuñez outside Acla, when he was on his way from the shores of the South Sea, obeying the summons of Pedrarias. He afterwards accompanied Pedrarias to Panama, served in various expeditions, and received a grant of land on the Chagres river.

[1] Scarcely anything is known of Almagro until he appears on the scene as the partner of Pizarro, in this daring project. (See my translation of *Alonzo Enriquez*, note at p. 134.)

[2] Hernando de Luque had been a schoolmaster at Darien, and was a priest in Panama. He owned the island of Taboga, and had amassed considerable wealth. (*Commentarios Reales*, ii, lib. i, cap. i.) He died just before Pizarro obtained the enormous ransom from the Ynca Atahualpa, and for that reason his portion of the spoils was not set apart. (*Com. Real.* ii, lib. i, cap. 28.)

[3] They held their grants of land on the banks of the river Chagres in partnership, where they raised cattle, and realised a considerable sum of money. The licentiate Espinosa was also in the partnership.

[4] The agreement between the partners was dated March 10th, 1526. Pizarro and Almagro could not write. One Juan de Panes signed for Pizarro, and Alvaro del Quiro for Almagro. Pizarro was then fifty-six years of age. When Pedrarias was superseded, he retired from the partnership, to which he had never contributed a farthing.

which I had subdued, where he began to provision his ship. He was in an open road on this coast, with very lofty mountains rising up close to the sea, so that there was no land breeze to take the ship off the coast. The wind was continually from the west, and they were nearly four years in reaching the island of Gallo on that coast, where more than four hundred men died on the beach. Pedrarias and Almagro sent such reinforcements as they could collect from Panama.[1]

This province of Birú is bordered, on the upper coast, by the territory of two chiefs who had come as conquerors from the neighbourhood of Darien, and subdued the land. They are Caribs, and use arrows poisoned with a very evil plant. They are named Capucigra and Tamasagra, and are rich in gold. The people of Birú, as a defence against their arrows, make shields through which no arrow can pass; but nevertheless, as their dreaded enemies eat human flesh, those of Birú fear them infinitely.

Though it appeared from my report that these chiefs were rich, I nevertheless advised that Pizarro should not touch there, lest he should be lost, but that he should sail on from Panama on the high sea. But he went to Birú, where the Indians came down to the coast in an orderly way, wishing to treat for peace. Certain Indians, also, came to the Spanish camp, saying, that if the Spaniards wanted to trade, they were ready. Thus they began to ask for things of little value from the Spaniards, offering much in return. Pizarro, not knowing how best to deal with them, ordered that no one should traffic with them on pain of severe punishment. When the Indians saw that the Spaniards were not traders, they took up their arms and retired into their village. Pizarro marched to it, and found

[1] Pizarro sailed in the middle of November 1524. As many as twenty-seven Spaniards died at Puerto de la Hambre, in Andagoya's land of Birú, and, as Andagoya says, the fourth year had commenced before Pizarro discovered Peru. He returned to Panama in 1528.

that it was on a height, where it could not be stormed. Some of the Indians, who had been brought by the Christians to cut grass for the horses, were hit by arrows, and twelve days afterwards they were swollen like barrels.

Pizarro now saw that he had been well advised not to touch at this place. He passed on to the island of Palmas, where he found eight or ten houses, maize, and other provisions. Here he remained some days, and the Indians attacked him, and wounded some Spaniards. He sailed on, and, without touching at the port of Buenaventura, arrived at a province which is bounded by the river of San Juan. Here the Indians killed some Spaniards. Not being able to go inland, Pizarro sailed on past the river of San Juan, at the mouth of which they came to a village, where they found eleven or twelve thousand *castellanos*. Having robbed this village they passed on, without touching at any point until they came to the island of Gorgona, and as this was uninhabited, they went on to the island of Gallo.

And before they reached this island, they had taken the four years of which I spoke. At this time, Pedro de los Rios came to Panama as governor, who, moved by avarice, wished to displace Pizarro from the command of the expedition, and he sent a captain in search of him. This captain found the followers of Pizarro at Gallo, and he took them back, Pedro de los Rios having ordered that they should return to Panama.

Pizarro, seeing himself ruined by this, determined to remain there with ten[1] men, who wished to accompany him. He sent the vessels, with only the sailors on board, to search the coast a-head, and they reached as far as a land which was level and open. The vessels returned to the island of Gallo, where Pizarro had been for seven or eight months. Pizarro then sailed along this coast in the

[1] Thirteen. See an account of these intrepid men in a note at p. 419 of my translation of *Cieza de Leon*.

vessel, and discovered Tumbez and Payta. Here Pedro de
Candia[1] went on shore, and came to Tumbez, where he said
he had seen grand things, which did not afterwards appear.
The Indians, seeing that the Spaniards were so few in
number, did not fear them nor desire to injure them, thinking that they were merchants. Pizarro returned; and two
Spaniards remained on shore of their own accord, who, not
knowing how to conduct themselves towards the Indians,
were killed by them.[2] Pizarro returned to Spain with the
account of this discovery, and came back as governor. He
set out from Panama with a large force in two ships, and
landed on the island of Puna, which is opposite Tumbez.
This is an island inhabited by a populous and warlike race.
They came forth peacefully; and on learning what the
Christians intended, they attacked their camp at dawn one
morning, and put the Christians to great straits. They
wounded Hernando Pizarro, who fell from his horse. The
Indians being defeated and the island subdued, plenty of
provisions arrived at the camp; and Pizarro waited there,
without landing on the opposite coast, until Hernando de
Soto[3] arrived from Nicaragua with the other ships, and re-

[1] For an account of Pedro de Candia, see my *Cieza de Leon*, note,
p. 193.

[2] Only one, Alonzo de Molina, one of the thirteen who crossed the
line. He died before the return of Pizarro. *Herrera*, dec. iii, lib. iii,
cap. 3.

[3] Hernando de Soto was a native of Estremadura, son of a gentleman
of Xeres de Badajos. He went to America in the expedition of Pedrarias, and received promotion from him. Almagro sent him with a ship
to Nicaragua to collect troops and arms, and he sailed thence to reinforce
Pizarro, whom he found on the island of Puná, on the point of com-
mencing the invasion of Peru. In May 1532 Hernando de Soto landed
with Pizarro at Tumbez, and took a leading part in the subsequent conquest. He was one of Pizarro's most enterprising lieutenants. He was
absent when the Ynca Atahualpa was so basely murdered by Pizarro and
his vile crew, and it is highly to his credit that, on his return, he ex-
pressed the greatest indignation at the perpetration of this atrocious act.
He went in advance of Pizarro, to Cuzco, but soon afterwards returned

inforcements of men and horses. When the reinforcements arrived, which enabled him to go inland, Pizarro went to Tumbez, and treated for peace with the chief of that place. He then founded the town of San Miguel, at Payta, the site of which was afterwards removed upwards of twenty leagues, to the place where the town now stands, the district being healthier and more convenient. Leaving this town with a few settlers in it, Pizarro went in search of Atabalica,[1] who was lord of the whole country. He arrived in the province of Cajamalca, where he found Atabalica. Pizarro had to pass through a gorge in the mountains, and Atabalica was informed of his approach, but he would not oppose the passage of the Spaniards, as he might have done, saying, that he would allow them to cross the mountains, because afterwards they would not be able to escape, and he could then capture them all, and discover what manner of people they were.

Having descended to where Atabalica was encamped, they found him with a large body of men, in tents, outside the town. Pizarro wished to treat with him peaceably; so he sent the captain, Soto, on horseback, armed only with his

to Spain with his share of the ransom of Atahualpa, which made him a rich man. He married a daughter of Pedrarias, and was appointed governor of Cuba and adelantado of Florida. The expedition commanded by Hernando de Soto sailed from Seville in 1538, and reached Cuba in safety. Leaving his wife Isabella at Havanna he sailed for Florida in May 1539, and landed on the coast. Then followed his wonderful march through the modern States of Georgia and Alabama, and his discovery of the Mississippi. His Portuguese biographer says: " On May 21st, 1542, departed out of this life the virtuous, and valiant captain Don Hernando de Soto, governor of Cuba, and adelantado of Florida, whom fortune advanced, as it used to do others, that he might have the higher fall." His companions wrapped his body in his mantle, with a great deal of sand, and cast it into the mighty Mississippi. Hernando de Soto was the equal of Vasco Nuñez for indomitable courage and perseverance, but, like most of these Spanish conquerors, he was detestably cruel.

[1] The Ynca Atahualpa.

tongue. Soto forced on his horse when he arrived at the
place where Atabalica was seated on his throne, until he
was close to him. Atabalica showed no sign of fear, and
did not even rise. Soto then delivered his speech, saying
how they came there on the part of the King of Spain, and
that they wished to be friends. He replied, that they
should lodge in the town, and that he would come and see
them there. He did this that he might secure them all in
the town. When Soto left him, there were large bodies
of troops on each side of the road, and when Soto came
near them on horseback, they got out of the way with
some show of fear. When Atabalica saw it, he ordered
their heads to be cut off, saying that they had no reason
to be afraid when he was there, and that they had fled from
a sheep.

On another day Atabalica, putting his forces in order,
advanced to the town where Pizarro was, in his litter, without considering it necessary to alight from it. He entered
Cajamalca, where the Spaniards were lodged in the houses.
The cavalry knew what was to be done, if Atabalica
should not desire peace. Fray Vicente de Valverde, who
was afterwards Bishop of Cuzco, came out to receive Atabalica, with a breviary in his hands, saying certain things
concerning the power of God. Atabalica took the book
in his hand, and cast it away among the people, asking
how they had dared to enter his house to lodge in it?
Upon this the friar fled, and the troops, both horse and
foot, came out, and as the Indians had already entered the
open square, the cavalry charged them, and put them to
flight. Pizarro came up to Atabalica with the servants and
pulled him out of his litter, making him a prisoner. Atabalica, being captured, he surrendered the country, and
willingly became a vassal of his Majesty. He treated for his
ransom, for which he agreed to give a house (one of his
palaces) filled with gold and silver,—an undertaking which
he presently fulfilled.

Atabalica had a war with his brother, the lord of Cuzco. Guanacaba,[1] who was lord of all these lands, conquered and subdued the country from Cuzco, as far as Puerto Viejo, Quito, and other grand provinces; and this Guanacaba was so great an administrator that, when he conquered a province, he obliged its chief to go and live in Cuzco, make his home there, and cause his son and heir to serve as a page. And when any province made so strong a resistance as that its chief was killed, the people of that province were sent to live in the province of Cuzco, and some of those of Cuzco had to go to the conquered province, thus exchanging lands and villages, so that in no future time might there be a rising.[2] He placed his governors in these lands, and took the legitimate daughters of the chiefs of all the provinces for his women. The sons he had by them became lords of those provinces, so long as they recognised the lord of Cuzco as their superior.

Atabalica was son of Guanacaba, by the daughter of the lord of Quito, a very populous province, and a very pleasant. When Guanacapa died, his son, Guazcar,[3] became lord of Cuzco, and was saluted as Ynga, with ceremonies similar to those used in crowning a king or swearing in a prince. Before these ceremonies are performed, he is not lord, but he must be shut up in a palace, and remain there certain days, fasting, and doing other things; and he must not see a woman during this time. Having complied with these obligations, they bring him forth with great solemnity, and place a fringe, in place of a crown, on his brow, made of various coloured wool, gold and silver, very rich. No other man may put on this fringe, not even the captain-general, on pain of death.

[1] The Ynca Huayna Ccapac.
[2] For an account of the Ynca institution of *Mitimaes* or colonists, see *Cieza de Leon*, pp. 149, 150, 209, 328, 362.
[3] The Ynca Huascar.

E

Having received the title of Ynga, which is the same as
king, he sent to all his brothers, each one of whom was lord
of a province, ordering them to come to acknowledge him,
as was their duty. Atabalica was a proud and wilful man,
and he replied that he was as much the son of Guanacaba
as the lord of Cuzco himself, that he would not recognise
his sovereignty, but that, on the contrary, he intended to
enter Guazcar's dominions, and make himself master of
Cuzco. Guazcar, on the receipt of this message, sent an
army against his brother, and Atabalica came forth to give
battle, but was taken prisoner by the captains of Guazcar,
and a great number of people were killed.

The captains of Cuzco were given a city in the territory
of Atabalica, called Domipumpa,[1] in which Atabalica was
imprisoned, within a tower, with certain captains. But he
made a passage under the foundations, got out, and reached
Quito. As soon as he escaped, he called his people together
at Quito, and collected an army again. The others came
against him ; but by means of a warlike stratagem, he defeated them, and killed or captured nearly all. He then
marched against the city where he had been imprisoned,
and when the garrison saw him approach in great anger,
fifty of the principal old men came out, and threw themselves at his feet, praying for mercy. But he refused to
hear them ; and entering the city, he killed over seventy
thousand souls. It was a punishment which was feared
wherever he went conquering. Thence Atabalica advanced
to Cajamalca, and extended his army to Jauja and Chincha.
When he had conquered these provinces, he marched towards
Cuzco. Guazcar came forth, holding his enemy cheap, with
his *Orejones*, who were the knights, and all very valiant
men. These were of the tribe of Cuzco. They joined
battle, and there was great slaughter on both sides.
Through the ardour of one of Atabalica's captains, named

[1] Tuma-pampa.

Puricachima,[1] the Inga was taken prisoner. Fearing that the followers of the Inga would rescue him, he treated with the Inga concerning his release, and proposed that all his captains should come to confer about it, giving many good reasons. When the captains came, trusting to the word of Puricachima, he seized them all, and cut off their heads.[2] Thus he entered Cuzco, and was its master; and taking the captive chief and his treasure, he set out on his return to Cajamalca, where Atabalica was. But when the messengers of Puricachima and Quizquiz arrived, they found that Atabalica was already a prisoner in the hands of Pizarro,—for he was himself a captive before Guazcar was taken prisoner.

When it was known in the camp how Atabalica had been made prisoner, and by what sort of people, and that a house of gold and silver was required for his ransom, it came to the ears of Guazcar, who said, "How shall my brother get so much gold and silver for himself; I would give twice as much as he can, if they would kill him, and leave me as lord." This saying was told to Puricachima, who presently sent a messenger to Atabalica to tell him what his brother had said. Then Atabalica went to the governor, feigning grief, and saying, that he had received news that his brother had been killed by the captain who had taken him prisoner. As Pizarro was ignorant of the deceit, he tried to console his prisoner by saying that he should not be sad, for as his brother was dead, there was nothing to be done. Atabalica, having thus found out that Pizarro would not harm him if his brother was killed, sent messengers to his captains with orders to cut off Guazcar's head.

Having done this, and collected the ransom, Atabalica found that, as a pretext to kill him, or from fear that, being

---

[1] Chalcuchima.

[2] For an account of the war between Huascar and Atahualpa, see *Cieza de Leon*, p. 273 and note.

free, he would rise against them, the Spaniards had made
Indian sorcerers, who bore ill-will against Atabalica, declare
that he had an army ready to kill them. Atabalica replied
that it was a lie, and that they might rest satisfied that no
Indian would move throughout the land without his order.
He said, that when they saw anything suspicious, then they
might kill him; and that to satisfy themselves they should
send some one to the plain where it was said that the army
was, to ascertain the truth of the story. For this purpose, Captain Soto set out with some followers, and as it was arranged
between Pizarro and his councillors, they killed Atabalica
before the return of Soto. And at the time of his death he
said many things concerning the pledge which had been
broken.

Atabalica was so perfect a gentleman that, when playing
at chess with a Spaniard, he staked cups of gold against
something from Spain. If he won, he did not take what
the Spaniards had put down, but he gave up his own
stakes promptly. One day the governor ordered these cups
to be taken and put into the house of deposit; and when
Atabalica knew this, he asked why the winnings of his
opponents were put there; that his opponent ought not to
have reason for thinking that he had not fulfilled his agreement; that what the man had won should be returned to
him, lest he should believe that he, Atabalica, was not a
great lord.

As soon as Atabalica was dead, Pizarro set out for the
province of Jauja, and founded a city, which, owing to
its distance from the sea-coast, was afterwards removed to
the province of Lima, where now stands the City of the
Kings. From Jauja, the adelantado Almagro and Soto
departed for Cuzco, and taking the spies who were on the
road, they suddenly attacked the army of Cuzco, defeated
it, and following closely, entered Cuzco after the Indians.
Thus Cuzco was taken, and the city which is now called
Cuzco was founded for his Majesty.

After these lords were dead (Atabalica and Guazcar), Pizarro raised up their brother, a youth who was with him, to be lord and Inga; and this youth, owing to the ill-treatment he had received, rebelled, and marched with a large army against Cuzco, which he besieged for three months.[1] During this time he often occupied half the city, and in retaking the fortress, Juan Pizarro was killed. He also sent an army against the City of the Kings, which was besieged. Before the siege commenced, Pizarro sent three or four detachments to succour Cuzco, under Diego Pizarro and Gonzalo de Tapia; but these two captains, with all their people, were killed by the Indians, and not one escaped. They also defeated Morgobajo in Jauja, and killed most of his followers, the rest escaping by flight.

The adelantado Don Diego de Almagro had departed from Cuzco with six hundred Spaniards and a great many Indians. Villavina,[2] who was a brother of the Inga, and whom the Indians looked upon as a pope, went with him. He marched to the provinces of Chile, which were within his government, and not finding in that land the means of founding settlements where Spaniards might live, and learning from the Indians that their brethren had taken Cuzco, and that the Spaniards in it were killed, he returned to Cuzco. When he got there he found that the Indians had given up the war on receiving news of his approach. He found Hernando Pizarro in Cuzco, to whom he sent to announce his arrival. He said that he must receive him, because that city was within his government. Hernando Pizarro denied this. Finally, Almagro entered Cuzco in spite of Hernando Pizarro, who retreated into a house and barricaded it; but he was captured. Almagro then commenced a suit against him for having been the cause of the rising of the Inga, and for other misdoings. But through

[1] The Ynca Manco.
[2] The "Huillac Umu," or high priest: a brother of the Ynca Manco.

tho intorvontion of others, Almagro thought it well to
bring Hernando to Chincha, where the governor, Pizarro,
was, and there he was set free on certain conditions. As
soon as he was free, not only did he not keep the agreement that had been made between them, but he wished to
seize Almagro, who returned to Cuzco, and the Pizarros
began to collect troops to march against him. Then Hernando Pizarro gave battle to the followers of Almagro, near
Cuzco, and, through the fault of certain captains, Almagro
was defeated and taken prisoner, and Hernando Pizarro,
proceeding against him, put him to death.

Don Francisco Pizarro now held the whole country in his
own possession. He founded a town at Aliquapa,[1] which is
a port of the sea for Cuzco, and another town at Guania-
gaques, in the province of Jauja; and between the City of
the Kings and San Miguel he founded Trujillo, under which
is placed the province of Cajamalca, and other neighbouring districts. On the borders of Trujillo, in the interior,
there is a province called Brocamaros, where Alonzo de
Alvarado went to make a conquest, by order of Pizarro,
and there he made a settlement. They say it is a rich and
populous district. Don Diego de Almagro was the first
who founded a town in the province of Quito, called Santiago. He went there to resist the invasion of the adelantado
Don Pedro de Alvarado, who had embarked at Puerto Viejo
with a strong force, and had taken the road to Quito.
Having come to the encampment of Almagro, they agreed
together, and Almagro gave Alvarado one hundred thousand
castellanos in exchange for his troops and ships. Wishing
to go to the City of the Kings to see Pizarro, he left Benalcazar
in Quito as captain. This captain abandoned Santiago and
founded San Francisco, which is now the chief place in that
province. At that time Pizarro sent men to form a settlement at Puerto Viejo, and afterwards another town was

[1] Arequipa.

founded, called Santiago,[1] opposite to the Island of Puna. But the Indians of Puna attacked it, killed those who were in it, and laid it waste.

The first lord, of whom there was any recollection in Cuzco, was the Inga Viracoche.[2] This was a man who came to that land alone; but there is no record of whence he came, except that Viracoche, in the language of the people, means "Foam of the sea." He was a white and bearded man, like a Spaniard.[3] The natives of Cuzco, seeing his great valour, took it for something divine, and received him as their chief. He ordained many excellent laws and regulations for the government of the land; built the edifices of Cuzco and the fortress, which is made in a wonderful manner. There is not much recollection of the successors of this chief down to Guanacaba, because they were not men who merited it. Guanacaba, on coming to the throne, commenced a career of conquest, and his valour was so great that he subdued the country as far as Puerto Viejo in a northern direction, and to Chile on the south. He was the best governor of whom there is any memory. He made a very broad road from Cuzco to the entrance into Quito, with a wall on each side; and it is carried so well over the mountains, and so well paved throughout, that it appears like a Roman work. By this road the flocks of sheep went, laden with merchandise, from one part to another. All along this road, and along others which led to other parts, they had post-houses placed at a distance, such as an Indian might run without being tired. And they had Indians so swift that this running-post could not be equalled by any horse-post. When any tidings had to be sent, or anyone was to be despatched to a distant province, the first post received the message, and when the runner came in sight of another post, he called out the message

---

[1] The modern Guayaquil.   [2] The Ynca Huira-ccocha.
[3] See *Cieza de Leon*, p. 357.

to another runner, who started at once for the next post; and thus news was brought from all parts of the land, and the proceedings of the captains in every province, on each day, were known. Each captain had an army, according to the importance of his province, in order that any disturbance might at once be punished. The pay received by the soldiers consisted of all things necessary for themselves, their wives, and children, as well food as clothing. In each province, where an army was stationed, there was a store-house full of all kinds of clothing and arms; and though the cost was great, these houses were always kept full of the things which the natives of the different provinces had to provide for the men of war. These soldiers never entered a village; they had their tents in the fields, and took their wives and children with them; and thus, without paying them other wages, the Ingas kept their armies always in the field. When a province was conquered, the *Orejones* were sent to it as governors and collectors of tribute. They kept so good a record in the provinces, that they knew how many were born and how many died each year; and by means of knots they could reckon every sum that can be reckoned with a pen. The number of sheep that was reared in that country was wonderful; and the traffic from the sea to the inland districts, and from one province to another, was so great that there were many flocks of three hundred and two hundred together, laden with merchandise. When a province was taken, many sheep were provided to be reared there; so that in every province there were flocks of sheep, although before these provinces were conquered, there might not have been any. It was ordered, on pain of death, that the inhabitants of all the subject provinces should learn the language of Cuzco, and not speak any other, for originally they spoke different languages. Thus, the language of Cuzco was spoken over more than five hundred leagues. This was one of the excellent things in the Inga's government. It was also ordered that all the chiefs should reside at the court of Cuzco, and have the principal houses there. Thus the city became very great, while the provinces were secure and at peace, because their chiefs were living at the capital. When a chief died, his house, and wives, and servants remained as in his lifetime, and a statue of gold was made in the likeness of the chief, which was served as if it had been alive, and certain villages were set apart to provide it with clothing, and all other necessaries. The successor made a new house, and service of gold and silver, for it was not the custom to use those of his father. Thus there are great treasures which have not been discovered; for of those of Guanacaba, nothing has come into the hands of Christians.

The rites and ceremonies which prevailed in this land were the belief in the sun as a divine thing, to which they made sacrifices and offerings. And the order of their worship is that, when the sun rises, they bring many jars of *chicha* (which is the wine they make) into the open square of the city, and there they pour it out with certain ceremonies, placing their hands in front of their faces, and saying certain words. They had certain houses of the sun where they kept virgins, who were called women of the sun; and they lived in those houses like nuns, and kept from intercourse with men. He who attempted to do anything to them suffered death. These virgins had their services provided. If any of them appeared to be pregnant, she said it was by the sun, and this was believed, unless there was any evidence to the contrary.

The Ingas had excellent laws for the government and administration of justice, among which there was one that he who should take a woman in adultery, might kill both her and the man with whom she was taken. The climate of Cuzco is cold, with severe winters of snow and rain. That of Lima is temperate, and rain has never been known either there, or in any part of that coast, from Erguita[1] to San Miguel, because the same winds blow throughout the year. Therefore the houses built by the Indians were more for protection from the sun than from rain. They had houses of the sun where there were certain statues of gold, and the pillars, bolts, and doors were all of gold and silver in great quantity. The people of that land were well versed in weights and measures; and they were great workers in silver, after their fashion. Guanacaba was so strict concerning the houses of gold and silver which he built, that the worker in those metals who did not do his work as it was ordered, died for it. Besides the tribute which was given to this lord, he had great mines of gold and silver.

No lord, however great he might be, entered the presence of the Inga in rich clothing, but in humble attire and bare-footed, and with some offering which he carried on his shoulders; though he had come to the presence in a rich litter of silver and gold. Nor might any man look at the Inga's face but with eyes down and very humbly. The shirt which the Inga had once worn, was never used again, nor the cup nor the plate. They had extremely grand and strange usages.

From San Miguel towards Puerto Viejo and the north the climate changes; for it rains in certain seasons, and the heat is greater. The people too are very different. They go to sea to fish, and navigate along the coast in *balsas* made of light poles, which are so strong that the sea has much ado to break them. They carry horses and many people, and are navigated with sails, like ships. In these provinces are found the rich emeralds which are met with throughout the land. On the coast there

---

[1] Arequipa.

is a fountain of rosin, whence they take a rosin like tar,
and it forms a little lake in front of the fountain which
gives it birth, and there it thickens under the sun. The
ships which pass by, take quantities on board, and with
it they tar the ropes and the ship's sides. On this
coast there are salt deposits within the water of the sea,
where the ships that pass take in cargos. The Indians of
that land, owing to the slight resistance it offers, cut it out
in blocks, and these blocks are of very excellent salt. From
Tumbez onwards to Cuzco the land is so destitute of trees
that in many parts of the road no place can be found to tie
up a horse. Besides the sheep there are plenty of deer,
partridges, and other birds, different from those of Spain.
The land is so rich and fertile that from the first *escudilla*
of wheat they sowed at Lima, they reaped eight hundred,
and from one *fanega*[1] they got eight hundred; and generally
they reap three hundred to four hundred from one. All the
products of Spain yield wonderfully.

The government of New Castille commences in the province of Catanez, which is north of Puerto Viejo, and extends to the river of San Juan. In the year 1536, this
government was given to the licentiate Gaspar de Espinosa,
who died at Cuzco in 1537, having gone to assist the
Marquis Don Francisco Pizarro, and intending to go thence
to his government.[2] This news arrived at court when I

[1] Porringer.

[2] The licentiate Gaspar de Espinosa went out with Pedrarias to
Darien as alcalde mayor in 1514. He it was who was ordered by the
cruel old governor to sit in judgment upon Vasco Nuñez, the great discoverer of the South Sea, whom he knew to be innocent. He reluctantly
found him guilty, but recommended him to mercy on the ground of
his great services, urging that at least he should be allowed to appeal.
Soon afterwards the licentiate was sent on that expedition in which
Andagoya accompanied him, and during which he committed many
atrocities on the Indians. He also went in the vessels built by Vasco
Nuñez, as far up the coast of the South Sea as Cape Blanco, in Costa
Rica, in 1518. Espinosa amassed considerable wealth, and he supplied

was there, in the end of the year 1537, and a grant of this same government was made to me, from the point of San Juan to the gulf of San Miguel. I started from Toledo in the year 1538, and embarked at San Lucar in the beginning of 1539, taking sixty men with me from Spain. I arrived at Nombre de Dios on the day of San Juan, and began to prepare my expedition at Panama, having collected two hundred men. I was thus engaged until the 15th of February, having made three ships and two brigantines. I left Panama on the 15th of February, and doubling Cape Corrientes, sailed along the coast as far as the island of Palmas, where I disembarked all the men and horses. I found here five Indian huts, with some maize. I then sent the brigantines to seek the inhabited parts; but the land is so thick with trees, and overgrown with rushes which enter the sea, that there were no inhabitants found, except those of the five huts, and these came from the banks of a river to this island to fish. Eight leagues from this island, the port of Buenaventura was discovered, and a road descended through a very dense forest to the sea, by which the Indians came to get salt. The Indians came down by these forest-covered mountains, which are the highest and most rugged that have been seen in the Indies. Leaving fifty men with the ships, I entered this road with all the rest of the men and horses, which I conveyed to a distance of nine leagues from the sea with great labour; but from that point onwards the country was and is so rugged that many dogs, not being able to go on with the men, returned to the sea. At a distance of fourteen leagues from the sea

most of the funds to Luque, the partner of Pizarro and Almagro in the conquest of Peru. In 1537 he arrived at Lima with reinforcements for Pizarro, which he had collected in Panama, Nombre de Dios, and Tierra Firme; and Pizarro immediately sent him as his envoy to Almagro at Cuzco, where he died. It appears, from Andagoya's narrative, that he had previously been appointed to the government of New Castille by the court of Spain.

I came to a province called Atanzeta, a very rugged country, but well peopled. The Indians came out prepared for war, but as we gave no occasion for it, and entered their villages without seizing or robbing anyone, they all became friendly. Here I learnt that, in a province called Lili, ten leagues further on, there was a town of Christians, which Belalcazar left there when he departed from this land.[1] The town is called Cali, and was subject to the Marquis Don Francisco Pizarro. On the 10th day of May, 1540, I arrived at this town, and found thirty men in it, eighteen of whom were disabled. I learnt how the Indians of a province, ten leagues distant, had killed the captain, Pedro de Añasco, and the captain Osorio, with upwards of fifty Spaniards, and as many horses, and were besieging a town called Timana, which Pedro de Añasco had founded.[3] The besieged had sent for help to the captain Juan de Ampudia, who was at Popayan, and he had sent to pray for succour from Lili. The force which was prepared to set out from these two towns of Popayan and Lili amounting to sixty men. Two days after I arrived at Lili,[4] news arrived how that the Indians had defeated and

---

[1] Andagoya marched to Cali through such ways that all his horses were killed, and his men were much harassed. Herrera says that " Andagoya had a commission from the king to conquer the country round the Rio de San Juan, but he landed in a bay, and marched to Cali, without considering that there is no Rio de San Juan in all that country." *Herrera*, Dec. iv, lib. v, cap. 3.

[2] See *Cieza de Leon*, pages 93, 96, 99.

[3] Osorio and Añasco were making their way from Popayan to Bogota by the river Paez, when they were attacked and killed by the Indians with all their party. Juan de Ampudia marched out of Popayan to resist these Indians, and routed them three times, but they still continued to attack him, and he was killed in the fourth encounter. His men escaped to Popayan under cover of night. *Herrera*.

Pedro de Añasco of Seville was a brother-in-law of Alonzo Enriquez. (See my *Life and Acts of Alonzo Enriquez*, p. 48.) He was engaged in a street brawl with him. His brother Juan de Añasco was second in command with Hernando de Soto, when he discovered the Mississippi.

[4] Cali and Lili appear to be the same place. Cali is the town, and

killed Juan de Ampudia, with other soldiers; that the survivors were flying by night through the forests; and that the Indians, following up their success, had appeared before Popayan. I made haste to march and resist their entry, and on my arrival they halted. As soon as I arrived at Popayan, I sent a captain, with fifty arquebusiers and cross-bowmen, by a secret road, to succour Timana, and they arrived at a time when the greater part of the inhabitants were on the road, with the intention of going to Bogota. Thus I restored peace to the province of Popayan.[1]

This Juan de Ampudia and Pedro de Añasco set out from Quito in the year 1536, with the troops that had been left there by Don Pedro de Alvarado, and marched through this province until they arrived at Lili, where Juan de Ampudia formed a settlement, which he called the town of Ampudia. In 1538, Belalcazar marched against them from Quito, in disobedience of the express orders of his governor. When he arrived in Lili, he caused the town which Juan de Ampudia had formed, to be abandoned, and founded Cali and Popayan. In 1539, as soon as Belalcazar heard that the licentiate Espinosa was governor of that land, he abandoned those two towns, with few men in them, and went thence to the province of Bogota, where he found the licentiate Jimenez and Filaymana,[2] captains from Santa Martha and Venezuela. Leaving a brother of the licentiate Jimenez there as captain, they all went on to Spain.[3]

Lili the Indian district, in the valley of the Cauca. See *Cieza de Leon*, pp. 101, 104, 93, 96, 99, 103.

[1] " Andagoya possessed himself of Popayan, and fearing that Belalcazar, who had founded this place, would return and call him to account, he connived at all the crimes that were committed, to ingratiate himself with the inhabitants, that they might assert his unjust cause." *Herrera.*

[2] Nicholas Fedreman, a German knight and lieutenant of the German governor of Venezuela, George of Spires.

[3] For an account of the meeting of Quesada, Fedreman, and Belalcazar at Bogota, see my Introduction to the *Search for El Dorado*, p. x.

The Marquis Don Francisco Pizarro, when he heard that Belalcazar had risen against him, sent the captain, Lorenzo de Aldana,[1] as his lieutenant, with an order to arrest Belalcazar, and bring him to Lima; but Aldana found that he had already left the country. While Lorenzo de Aldana was in Lili, in 1539, the licentiate, Badillo,[2] arrived there from Carthagena, in search of Peru. Badillo saw that his enterprise was at an end, because the land which he had reached was already occupied by Christians; so leaving a part of his followers in Lili, he went on through Quito, embarked at Payta, and reached Santo Domingo. Lorenzo de Aldana learnt from Badillo that he had passed through a rich and populous country, and that, at a distance of forty leagues, there was a country called Birú (the same which I discovered from Panama). So, in the same year of 1539, Aldana sent Jorge Robledo with an expedition to that province, and another captain came from Carthagena in search of Badillo. When Robledo heard that other Spaniards were coming, he founded a town, which he called Santa Ana, although he had not received powers to form settlements. The next day, those of Carthagena arrived where he was, and finding officers of justice, they put themselves under their protection. Then the captain, and as many as chose to follow him, went on to Lili, restoring peace and security to the province of Popayan.[3]

I sent a captain to these provinces in search of Jorge Robledo, because his position was not known; and the captain arrived at this settlement, where there were thirty men with five horses, and the chiefs of the country were about to attack them. Jorge Robledo had crossed to the other side of the great river, and had gone down it, no one

[1] See *Cieza de Leon*, p. 123.

[2] Juan de Vadillo. See *Cieza de Leon*, pp. 40, 47 note, 50, 53 note, 57, etc.

[3] Cieza de Leon was a man at arms serving under Vadillo and Robledo; and a full account of all these events is given in his *Cronica*.

know whither. My captain was received in the settlement
by the Spaniards, who gave thanks to God that he had come
to their relief at such a time. Leaving the troops there,
the captain returned to report to me that there were no
tidings of Jorge Robledo. Soon after, as Jorge Robledo
returned along the same road that he had gone by, he
arrived at a province called Camboya, seventeen leagues
from the settlement where he had left the Christians. Here
he heard how that I was governor of that land. I had
ordered the town of Santa Ana to be founded, as it was
within my jurisdiction ; and as I was already in the country
when Jorge Robledo founded it, I ordered it to be named
San Juan.[1] Jorge Robledo departed, leaving his followers
in Timana, and came to Lili, where I was, reporting to me
what he had done. I then sent him as my lieutenant-
general to establish a city in that province, which I ordered
to be called Cartago ; and when this was done, to found
another town in the province of Boritica, where Antioquia
now stands.

On arriving at Lili, I found that the road by which I
came was so rugged that it was impossible for horses to
pass ; so I presently sent a party to discover another road
which should avoid the mountains. The new road came to
the seaside, in the bay of Zinzy (province of Yolo), where
I ordered the city of Buenaventura to be founded. On that
coast a large river opens out into a bay, three leagues
across, where ships, laden with all their cargo, may approach
so near the land as to disembark the horses in the very
square of the town. The land is wooded, and there are
many fruits ; and pig hunting. This city is twenty-two
leagues from that of Lili, east and west ; and that of Lili
is nearly twenty from that of Popayan, north and south.
Popayan is twenty-six leagues from the river of San Juan.

---

[1] As soon as Belalcazar arrived, and turned out Andagoya, he ordered
that the town should not be called San Juan, but Santa Ana. *Herrera*.

The town of Timana is twenty-six leagues east of Popayan ; and the town of Pasto, which was founded by the captain Pedro de Puelles,[1] under orders from the governor Francisco Pizarro, is thirty-eight leagues south of Popayan. Pasto is within my jurisdiction.

The province of Tunceta is the highest land of that country, on the south-west side, along the coast. It is a very rugged and forest-covered region ; but where it borders on that of Lili, there are beautiful valleys and plains. The language of Tunceta is very different from that of Lili, and they do not understand each other without interpreters. A league from Lili there is a chief on a great river called Ciaman, where they speak a different language, not understood by the people of Lili. And two leagues to the eastward, in the other chain of mountains, there are more chiefs, with a language different from that of Lili.

On the ten leagues of road towards Popayan there is another chief, called Jamindi, with another language ; and many villages with five hundred to eight hundred houses ; of which, when I arrived, no memory remained, except the ashes ; for all had been destroyed, and the inhabitants killed by Belalcazar. From the said chief's territory commences the language of Jitirigiti, which prevails in the maritime cordillera, towards the river of San Juan and the south sea, in the valleys ; but in the mountains there is a different language. From the point where this language commences, on the east side of the Cordillera, the language of Popayan prevails for ten leagues to the southward. From the tops of the mountains, towards Timana, there is a different language ; and there are many other languages in the two chains of mountains as far as Quito. Of the twenty leagues between Popayan and Lili, the ten nearest Popayan are over a cold country, where a fire is necessary ; and the ten towards Lili are over a warm country, with almost the

[1] See *Cieza de Leon*, pp. 187 and 283.

F

climato of Panama. The whole is a very beautiful land, with plains, rivers full of fish, and abundant hunting of deer and rabbits. This land, now laid waste, was a most populous and fertile country, abounding in maize, fruit, and ducks. When I arrived, it was so laid waste that there was not a duck fit to breed, to be found throughout the land; and where there were over one hundred thousand houses in the space of these thirty leagues, I did not find ten thousand men. And the principal cause of their destruction was that they received such evil treatment, without having faith kept with them. In Popayan, the Christians never sowed during the whole time they were there, having the crops of the Indians to live on, and they gathered these crops, and turned their pigs and horses into the fields. So the Indians determined not to sow, and there was no maize for eight months, which caused so great a famine that many ate each other, and others died. Belalcazar also took many out of the country.

The few that remained were friendly, and I wished to convert them to our holy faith, and to learn whether they had any religion. They had none whatever, and did not even worship the sun, like those of Cuzco. But they lived according to the law of nature, with great justice, like those of Tierra Firme. The dress of the women was like that of the women of Tierra Firme; but the men wore a garment of cotton of very bright colours, which covered their loins, after the manner of a cloak, from below the arms; only it is short. The first who were converted in Popayan were one hundred of the natives of that land, and fifty of those of Quito, who had come here with the Spaniards. Among them was one chieftainess, and two or three chiefs. They asked me many lively questions, saying, " Why had nothing of this been told them before, for it appeared a good thing ?" and " Why, if, as we declared, we had come to give them life and salvation, had we killed many of them with so much

cruelty?" They often disputed among themselves as to
what manner of people those could be who did so much
harm, saying " When we are dead, whom will they have to
serve them?" They delighted greatly to hear the things
concerning the creation of the world; for they themselves
have a tradition of Noe's flood, just as we have. But they
had no other information in this province concerning Him
who was able to cause the water to rise and cover the land.

Having already instructed these one hundred and fifty
converts in the essentials of our holy faith, not touching
on the passion and incarnation of our Lord, and other mys-
teries, but only on matters easy to be believed, I wished to
convince them that there truly was a God the Creator.
I put before them how they might behold the sun; that
it was a thing created for the use of man and of the world,
and how it was ordained that it should not stop; and in like
manner the moon. I showed them that neither the earth,
which was without life, nor the sun and moon, nor the first
man, could do anything of themselves; whence they might
truly believe that it was the Creator and Maker of all things
who is God, whom we must worship. I did not think it
right to baptise them on the first day, but let them pass
the night on these thoughts, intending to baptise them next
morning. When they came to be baptised, I asked them
if they remembered what I had said to them the day before,
and whether they believed it, and desired to do as God
commanded. They replied that they had not slept all night,
but had conversed concerning all that had been said to
them, holding it all to be good, and that they desired to
do as God willed. I then placed crosses of red cloth on
their shirts, and took them in procession to the church,
where they again asked to be baptised. Mass was solemnly
said, and having explained somewhat concerning it, they all
ate with me, and I ordered that the captains and officers of
his Majesty should serve them, at which they were asto-

nished. After eating, I gave them to understand that on
that day they had merited to be changed from beasts to sons
of God and heirs of his kingdom.   I ordered a tournament,
and a great festival to be celebrated, and they held it to be
very grand; and after four or five days there were three
hundred more, for whom the same festival was celebrated.

Having done this, I set out for the province of the Jitiri-
gites, which was four leagues off.   Here three conversions
were made in three different parts, and four or five thousand
persons were converted.   At one of the conversions, an
Indian turned to a captain, who was his master, when they
were learning the sixth commandment,[1] and said, "Well!
how is it that you have three wives?" The master, wishing
to dissimulate, did not answer, that I might not understand;
and when at last he said that they were not his wives, but
his servants; the Indian replied, "Then how is it that you
have them all with child?"   After the Indians were converted, the marriage state was treated of, and all the chiefs
were married according to law, and with a blessing.   There
was a woman, who had been three days married, from
whom a Spaniard solicited favours, which she would have
freely granted before her conversion.   But she replied,
almost rebuking him, " *Mana Señor que soy casada, y terna
Santa Maria ternan ancha pina;*"[2] which means, "do not
speak to me of such a thing, for I am married, and St. Mary
would be much offended."   In these provinces they worshipped the cross; and the lords ordered that any Indian
who passed by a cross should kiss and worship it, on pain
of punishment.   In one of these provinces, called Aisquis,
in the house of a chief named Jangono, on the day of

---

[1] The Catholics omit the second commandment as given in Exodus xx;
and so the seventh becomes the sixth. They make up the ten by dividing
the tenth into two.

[2] A mixture of Spanish and Quichua words. *Mana* (not), *ancha*
(very), *pina* (wrath), are Quichua.

Magdalen, following the conversion, treating of the marriage of a woman, whom they ought to take from the hand of God, they brought out beautiful fair women, who had never seen Spaniards, and were united that day. All the newly married couples dined with me, and I gave them all trinkets and ornaments of Castile. They were served at table in the same manner as those who were converted at Popayan. After dinner, the chief ordered twelve men to come with twelve flutes, who made very harmonious music. They all danced, and made the Spaniards dance with them. They passed the whole day dancing to this music; and at night they had many other games, inviting the Spaniards to play with them.

On my return to Popayan from these provinces there came to me the brother of a chief named Patia,[1] who lived at a distance of twenty or more leagues. Hitherto this chief had not been friendly; and the messenger said that his brother had sent him to tell me that he would have come himself, if he had not received a hurt out hunting. On the day of my entry into Popayan, I received messengers from this chief, who had been sent to give me welcome, and to say that he had learned how I had treated the chiefs and Indians, without deceiving them, and that for this reason he wished to be my friend, and to do as I desired. I sent back certain trinkets and ornaments by these messengers, to the chief, his wife, and some daughters he had. He sent his son to thank me, and I found him to be so intelligent and rational that I engaged in his conversion. He was converted, with his twelve Indians; and the same festival and solemnities were celebrated as on the former occasions, and they put on their crosses as signs that they were Christians. When he returned to his brother

---

[1] The Patia is a large river flowing into the Pacific. The valley of the Patia has a direction north and south, for a considerable distance, between Pasto and Popayan.

and lord, and gave an account of what had been done, the lord made festivals and rejoicings in the land.   When I sent eight men on horseback to the town of Pasto, with letters to be sent forward to the Marquis Don Francisco Pizarro; the chief learnt they were on the road, for they had to pass near his village.   His brother came out to receive them for nearly four leagues, with Indians and provisions, to escort them to the house of the chief, where no Spaniards had ever been before.   At a distance of nearly a league from the village, five hundred souls had come out, men and women, dancing and rejoicing, to conduct the Spaniards to the chief, who had made a great festival.   On their return, they came out to meet them again for four leagues, and induced them to tarry certain days in the village.   The chief then sent to ask me to come to his land, as he wished to become a Christian, with all his people. He engaged that all the neighbouring chiefs should do likewise, saying that they respected him, because he was a greater chief than they.

Having done all that was practicable in the way of conversion in these provinces, I returned to that of Lili, where they were very resolute in their refusal to hear or receive anything that was said to them.   At length the chief of that province had to come every morning to make me some houses, with his people, and he embraced me, and said that he was very fond of me.   I replied, that I also liked him very much, for he had served me better than the others, and therefore I liked him best.   I told him that if he wished to know God and become a Christian, I should like him better than my own son.   Fifteen days after I talked to him concerning these things, he came to me, crying out, that he wanted to be baptised, with all his people.   He and I agreed that the baptism should be performed three leagues from the town, where there was a large village.   At this conversion a servant of the chief, whose house was on a high mountain, came down with great diligence, with his children on his back. In telling these chiefs of the flood of Noe, they began to speak, and said that they held the same, having received it from their ancestors and grandfathers; and that they also held that there would be another destruction of the world by fire, and that afterwards there would be no more worlds. They said they believed all that was told them, because part of it was what they held. On pressing them with the questions why, if they believed these things, they did not consider who it was that could have power to destroy the world, and that no one could do this except He who made it? and why, if they understood this, they did not worship Him who was powerful to do this? They replied that they worshipped no one, and knew nothing more than what they had said: that all things in the world were made from heaven, and that they were ruled and governed from thence, but that they did not know who did this.

On another day of the conversion, mass was said, and a great cross was blessed. All the converted were present, numbering as many as six hundred souls, and they took the cross in procession, and placed it before the house of their chief. They worshipped it on their knees, as if they had seen it there all their lives. The servant of the chief was not there, being out purveying. When he returned, and entered the place where the chiefs were, they told him what had been done touching the adoration of the cross. He then went out alone, thirty men being seated in the open space where the cross stood, and, without saying anything, he passed us, went up to the cross, and fell on his knees, at a distance of four paces from it. In this position he went up to it and kissed it, then retired backwards a pace, rose up, and made a reverence with his whole body. He had a hooded cap in his hand, which he never put on until he had done all this. After rising from the place where he had adored

the cross, he stood gazing at it during the time you might
say a creed, and then passed to the right hand side of the
cross, where, without going on his knees, he worshipped
with an obeisance. He then went to another side and did
the same, and then to the left side, standing while you
might say a creed, and gazing. Having done this, he returned to where he had first worshipped, and, without
making an obeisance, he gazed during the time it would take
to say two creeds. Then he returned to us with great speed,
crying out twice, and pointing with his finger to St. Mary.

After this two chiefs, with twelve followers, came from
Lili de los Sierros, which extends from the other side of the
Rio Grande to within three leagues of the town of Lili.
When they came to the river they asked a chief, who was
there on an island, to supply them with fish. They besought
him also to put them across the river, offering to pay him,
saying that they were coming to see me, to which he con-
sented willingly. Having crossed over and come to his
houses, he seized and killed one of the chiefs, with six of his
followers, moved by avarice at the sight of the gold and salt
which they were bringing as a present to me. A Spanish
servant of mine, who came to visit this chief and to see
certain pigs that he had, found those men stretched on
mats, with their heads cut off, before the house of the
chief. When a boy asked what they were, the chief said
that there were as many more tied up in another house,
who were not dead. On appearing before me, I learnt what
had passed, and to whom those chiefs were coming. When
I asked them why they had come without being summoned,
they replied that they had heard how well their neighbours
were treated, and that, on hearing that news, they had
come to offer themselves to me. When that other chief
was made prisoner, he confessed what he had done before
the others, and his motive. After trial, he was sentenced
to death. Desiring to effect his conversion before the

execution, I had him brought before me from the prison, and it was more than an hour before he would answer a word. I left him and went out, and I did this three or four times, before he would reply to me. At last, God untied his tongue, and he replied to some things. Each hour after that, he was more inclined to attend to what was said, and I was with him from morning until evening. When at last he said that he wished to be a Christian, and to be baptised, I believed he did so that he might not be killed. I therefore told him not to become a Christian in the hope that he would not be put to death, because the sentence was already pronounced, but that he must do it that his soul might be saved. I told him to hold it for a certainty that if he should know and believe in God, and regret that he had not before known what had now been said to him, that then he would be born again to be for ever an heir to the kingdom of heaven, and that from a poor Indian he would become one of the greatest lords of the world; otherwise, he would die for ever in the pains of hell, concerning which he had been told. He replied with a very loud voice, and turning his face upwards, saying, that if he was to go to so good a Lord, he would die most willingly, and that his wife and children should also be baptised. This was done with great solemnity, and a cross being placed in his hands, without being untied, he said " Credo in Deo." Then, assisted by his relations, and by all the natives who were present, he was brought in procession to the open square where the gibbet stood. In tightening the cords they broke, and he fell to the ground unloosed; and before he got up, he sought for the cross which had fallen, and rose with it. When they were going to tie him again, he asked them to wait, and said there were two plates of gold under the bedplace in his prison, which should be secured, and that he would give them to me. He then told them to do as they pleased with him, and, saying the Creed, he died.

God wrought many other marvellous things in the conversion of this people; but to avoid being tedious, I will not repeat them here, except that, when I sent a captain to discover the coast, he entered a river with two brigantines. At one of the turns, they saw a great cross just erected. When the Spaniards saw the cross, knowing that no Christians had ever entered the river before, they rowed the brigantines so as to discover the turn of the river, and saw a canoe with six men coming away, who had just put up the cross. Further on there were two chiefs, with sixty other canoes waiting, who, when they saw the brigantines, made signs of peace. The captain replied to them, and a chief came to the brigantines in a canoe containing provisions. He asked the Spaniards, by signs, to come on shore to a great house that was there, and he went with them, and lodged them in it. This house was encircled on all sides by crosses. Wishing to know afterwards why they were received in this way by so warlike a people, for this is the province of the Peties, they found that these Peties were neighbours of those of Chasquio and of that chief Jangono, and that they traded with them. It appeared that some of the Peties, as spies, were present at the conversion, and saw all that was done with regard to the worship of the cross. For this reason, understanding all that we did, they came out to receive us with a cross.

This valley and district of Popayan is very beautiful and fertile. The provisions are maize, and certain roots called *papas*,[1] which are like chestnuts, and other roots like turnips, besides many fruits. But their chief provision is the wine which they make from maize in that land. It is made from a kind of maize called *niorocho*, a very small hard grain, which is reaped two months after sowing. They also make very good bread of it, and wine, honey, oil, and vinegar. In all the provinces of this government they have

---

[1] Potatoes.

these provisions, and in some of them they also have *aji*[1]
and *yucas*.[2] In Lili they do not eat the maize in the form
of bread, but toasted or boïled, although they have stones
on which to grind it. They make *chicha* ;[3] but their neighbours, who are the people of Atrinceta, eat their maize in
the shape of loaves of bread, for which reason they are a
stronger people than those of Lili.

These provinces have the same custom as those of Coiba
and Cueva, of celebrating festivals every year for their
dead. In these festivals those of one village united with
those of another, or the followers of one chief with those
of another, being friends, and ate and drank together, as is
done in Coiba and Cueva. After dinner, in the evenings,
they came out to play at tilting with reeds, a leader of one
side with fifty to thirty men, and another with as many
more, all with their shields well made and painted, and
their darts, which are the arms they carry in this country.
Having taken their places, they came out to skirmish, as
the troopers do in Spain, darting at each other like enemies,
and in this way they continued skirmishing, sallying forth
and retreating in skirmishing order, during the whole afternoon. Many came out from the game wounded, and some
were killed : and there was no penalty or ill feelings for
him who killed another. In the houses of the chief of
this province of Lili, they found, all round the principal
room, skins of men, as many as would fit into the room,
flayed and stuffed with cinders, and set up aloft at a height
of three or four *estados*.[4] They were seated close to each
other, with their arms placed in their hands as when living :
and the men of war ate those whom they captured and
killed, in token of victory.[5]

[1] *Capsicum frutescens.* The pepper used in almost all Peruvian dishes,
and called *uchu* in Quichua.
[2] *Jatropha Manihot.* (*Lin.*)   [3] A fermented liquor.
[4] An *estado* is a man's average height.
[5] For fuller details see *Cieza de Leon.*

In the chain of mountains overhanging the sea, whose waters flow into it, all is forest-covered and rugged, and there are villages as far as the shore. And from the river Santa Maria to near the island of Gallo, a distance of fifty leagues, brigantines may pass inland from one river to another, without going to sea, because one flows into the other. All the banks are inhabited, and the houses there are three hundred paces long by two hundred and eighty, and there are at least three hundred married people in each house. They all go in canoes, for there are no roads by land. They are made rich by trade in salt and by the fisheries. Opposite the island of Gallo there is a certain district where the banks of the rivers are well peopled. All the houses are fortresses, built over trees or on very high wooden pillars, and they go up by steps that can be put up or down. The people are rich, and not given to war, for it is enough that five or six men jump ashore from a boat, to frighten them away from their fortresses. Near this province there is a valley, nearly opposite the island of Gallo, called " de los Cedros," which is very populous and rich, and each house has its yard for the pigs of the country. The women have their arms covered with bracelets of fine gold in great quantity. News of the riches of this district and of the rites and ceremonies of the people have been received from all parts. No certain tidings have been received as yet from a captain I sent to settle the province of Catellez, and I do not know the name of the settlement he formed, so I do not put it down here.

There are many currents in this South Sea, for which reason it can only be navigated close in shore, except with long delay. They go up the coast every afternoon,[1] and (if possible) with the tide ; for there are many points where the wind alone does not suffice to stay the current.[2] The best

[1] Because the trade wind blows.

[2] Small sailing craft are sometimes driven back by the current, in front of the Talapazos.

time for navigating from Panama to Peru or Nicaragua is
from January to May, which is the season for north and
east winds ; but from Payta, and even from Puerto Viejo,
the wind is south all the year round. At the foot of Buenaventura the sea recedes more than half a league, and at the
island of Palms and the bay of La Cruz, it recedes the
distance of a cannon shot, though the distance from one of
these places to the other is eight and ten leagues. And all
along the coast the sea recedes more at one place than at
another, according to the flow. In the North Sea the tide
rises and falls very little, never more than half a cannon
shot, although there may be an ebb and flow between this
sea and gulf of Darien.

The province of Bogota bears east and west from Lili,
and is not distant above seven leagues on a straight road.
This province was very populous, and very rich in gold and
emeralds. The licentiate Jimenez and Federman set out in
search of Peru, and reached this province. When Federman arrived he found Jimenez already there, and that he had
founded a city called Santa Fé, and two other towns, the
names of which I do not remember. After Federman
reached the place where the licentiate Jimenez was established, Belalcazar joined them from Peru, and all three
agreed to depart, and went by the great river of Santa
Martha and Carthagena to this coast, and each one gave
the account which suited him. A brother of the licentiate
remained in Bogota as governor, and while he was there
Geronimo Lebron was placed at Santa Martha by the Audience of Santo Domingo, as governor, until His Majesty
should appoint another. As he of Bogota had been turned
out by the people and captains, Lebron desired that they
should receive him ; but they refused to comply, so he returned. This province was among the best, the richest, and
the most populous in the Indies, and as the captains were
not sure that they would not be turned out of their com-

mands, they only thought of enriching themselves. The
people were docile and friendly, and these captains did so
much harm to the land, and put so many Indians to death
for the purpose of robbing them, that the population has
greatly diminished. There are the same provisions in this
province as in the others, wonderful deer hunting, and the
climate is healthy, fresh, and temperate. There is a uni-
versal chief of all that land, who is very rich, and when he
saw the evil treatment his Indians had received, he neither
desired to be friendly nor to make war. This captain
Quesada, with the followers of Geronimo Lebron, and as
many more as he could collect, has gone inland, and up to
this time the result is not known.

There is a province called Apirama at a distance of ten
leagues from Popayan, which is where they killed the captains of whom I have already spoken. The chiefs of this
province, seeing that little resistance was made to their
invasion of Popayan, and that I had not been able to enter
their country to chastise them, waxed bold, and penetrated
within five leagues of the city of Popayan, laying waste the
land and killing the inhabitants they met with : so that it
became necessary to march against them, and invade their
country. I sent one hundred and fifty foot and sixty horse;
and they awaited their approach on a plain, formed in
close column, with as much precision as could have been
seen in Italy, to the number of twelve thousand, armed
with pikes forty *palmos* long, and between each pikeman
there was a man armed with a club which they call *macana*.
These came forth between the pikemen to fight, and then
retreated behind them; so that the cavalry could neither
break the line nor use their lances against them, until the
arquebusiers opened fire from a plain, and before the
Indians could close up they were charged by the cavalry.
Thus they suffered loss before they could retreat to rough
ground. After this they no more came down into the plains,

and in the mountains they practised warlike strategy by
which they wounded and surprised the cavalry who retired
to the camp, and in one skirmish they took three of my
soldiers alive. These chiefs hire Indians from other neighbouring provinces, called Tijajos, who hire themselves out
in all parts to any one who sends for them. This province
is to the eastward, between Popayan and Bogota. In
the cordillera of Popayan there are two or three volcanoes,
and there is snow on the tops of the mountains all the year
round.

When Mexico and all that land had been acquired, the
Adelantado Don Pedro de Alvarado went to the provinces
of Guatemala with all the troops he could collect in Mexico,
and those provinces were among the richest and most
populous in all this land. There was much resistance made
to him, and the Indians often fortified themselves in rocky
places. Alvarado committed many cruelties, and pacified the
land at great cost to the inhabitants. He took away many
people for the expedition he made to Peru, and made slaves
as in Nicaragua, so that there has been a great diminution
in the number of inhabitants in that land. It is a very
fertile and healthy country. This government contains the
city of Santiago, and the towns of San Salvador and San
Miguel, which is on the confines of Nicaragua. The people
of this land are like those of New Spain. In the year
1541, the Indians killed the Adelantado Don Pedro de
Alvarado, on his way from Mexico. At that time a mountain opened near the city of Santiago, and a river suddenly
flowed out, towards the city, with such fury that it tore up
trees that stood in the way. After doing much damage in
the country, it entered the city, and, leaving all other parts,
it flowed straight to the house of the said Adelantado,
where his wife was. It entered the house, so that not a
living thing was left that was not drowned or swept away.
Thus died his wife and all his family, except a daughter

who happened to be outside the house. The fury of the
river having passed, it remained without any water. Presently they entered the house to see what damage had been
done, and found a bull at the door of the chamber where
the Adelantado's dead wife was, with his horns down, and
he would suffer no one to enter; but this bull was never
seen more. The mountain opened near a volcano. In this
province there are the means of building ships, both timber
and all other materials; and there are abundant supplies of
provisions. On the death of the Adelantado, the licentiate
Maldonado remained in charge of the government.

The province of Carthagena is bounded on one side by
Santa Martha, and on the other by Darien. The first
governor who came there, after Pedrarias passed by that
coast, was Pedro de Heredia,[1] who was appointed governor
of the country from the great river of Santa Martha to that
of Uraba, for the purpose of gathering the Indians together
into towns, and bartering and treating with them, but not
for giving them as slaves to the colonists. This was the
cause of much mischief, for as no one held them, or thought
of having them in *encomienda*, so no one sought for them,
except to bring accusations against them, whereby to rob
and make slaves of them. When this mischief was amended,
there were few Indians who could cultivate the land; for the
country is sterile and unhealthy,—a low, swampy land, with
few rivers and little fresh water. The people, both men
and women, go quite naked; and they have few provisions,
but the fisheries are abundant. The people are the vilest
that I have seen anywhere.

The first town was formed at Carthagena, and afterwards
a town was founded in Uraba, near the great river of San
Sebastian. Another town is established at Mompox, near
the great river of Santa Martha; but this has always been
thinly settled; for the Indians killed certain Spaniards

[1] See *Cieza de Leon*, note at p. 35.

there. Some negroes, who had fled from the Christians, formed a village near Mompox, and served the Indians, and these negroes are now more feared in that land than the Indians.

In this land there is a province called Zenu, where, in ancient times, the Indians had their tombs, and above them great heaps of earth. All the Indians were buried with all the gold they possessed, of which much has been procured.[1] They have no rites nor ceremonies in this land.

The licentiate Badillo, a judge of Santo Domingo, came to take a *residencia* of Pedro de Heredia in the year 1536, and he kept Heredia a prisoner for a long time, until, at the request of Heredia, the licentiate Santa Cruz was sent out as *Juez de residencia* in the year 1537. When Santa Cruz arrived at Carthagena, he found that the licentiate Badillo had gone in search of Pirú, with all the men he could collect together, in a southerly direction. He passed by the province of Birú, which has already been described, and came to that of Lili, where he found the captain Lorenzo de Aldana, and here Badillo was dismissed, for most of his followers remained at Lili, while the rest went on to Quito. As soon as Santa Cruz arrived at Carthagena, he sent a captain after Badillo, with certain troops, who followed him as far as Lili, where the captain remained, and the troops went where they pleased.

Pedro de Heredia went to Spain with his *residencia* in the year 1539, and returned to the government of the province of Santa Martha. The first governor of Santa Martha was Bastidas, but one Villafuerte and another killed him by stabbing him in his tent, and he died before he could do anything permanent in that land. One Palomino then remained captain of the colony, who began to conquer the

___
[1] Becerra was sent by Pedrarias to discover this rich land of Zenu, where he lost his life. See page 27. In January 1534 Heredia, the governor of Carthagena, set out with a body of two hundred infantry

country, and had many encounters and wars with the Indians. He was so brave and valiant a man, that the Indians feared him, and began to come in peaceably. In crossing a great river on his horse, he was drowned. Afterwards Garcia de Lerma was appointed governor of that land.

There is a province, seven or eight leagues from the town and port of Santa Martha, inland, called Bonda, where there are large villages, but the country is very rugged and

and fifty cavalry, each with two or three spare animals, in search of Zenu. They marched inland through the dense forests, and at length reached a wide open plain, where the cavalry chased the deer. Here they came to some huts surrounded by a vast number of mounds or tumuli. This was the general cemetery of the surrounding country, where all the dead were buried, with their riches, food and drink. Heredia ordered the place to be pillaged. On the first day twenty-four wooden idols covered with gold plates, and some golden bells were collected. Heredia then marched further inland, in search of the place where the gold is found ; but the country was very difficult, his provisions were failing him, and he eventually retreated to Carthagena with an immense quantity of gold, in June 1534. Father Simon tells us that all who robbed these tombs died in extreme poverty.

The cemetery of Zenu was composed of thousands of tumuli, some conical, others oblong. When an Indian died, a hole was opened, large enough to contain the body, his arms and ornaments, with some jars of *chicha*, and heaps of maize, a stone for grinding it, and his wives and servants. The latter were first made drunk, and then buried alive. One mound was so large that the Spaniards discerned it at a distance of a league, and they called it the devil's tomb. Gold ornaments were found in almost all these tumuli. They were in the form of all kinds of animals, from a man to an ant, and 30,000 dollars' worth was taken from a single mound. The gold came from a great distance, and was obtained from other Indian tribes, by the men of Zenu, in exchange for hammocks, salt, and dried fish.

In recent times numerous gold ornaments have been dug up in the neighbourhood of the ancient Zenu, which possess considerable merit as works of art. See a description of some of them by Uricoechea. *Memoria sobre los Antiguedades Neo-Granadinos por Ezekiel Uricoechea*, p. 39. See also *Noticias Historiales de Fray Pedro Simon*, pte. iii, Not. i, No. 55, and *Descubrimiento de la Nueva Granada por El Coronel Joaquim Acosta*, cap. vii, p. 120. Cieza de Leon accompanied the expedition of Heredia to Zenu or Cenu, and mentions the immense quantity of gold found in the sepulchres. See my translation, pp. 221-8.

mountainous, the people warlike, and users of poisoned
arrows. Garcia de Lerma set out with a good force of
Spaniards to subdue them, but the Indians received the
invaders so well that they were defeated, and certain soldiers
were killed. Returning to their town, the Spaniards have not
again invaded that province. No other town was formed
in that province, and there was much trouble in subduing
it. There being some complaints against Garcia de Lerma,
the Dr. Infanta, a judge of Santo Domingo, arrived to take
his *residencia*, but in the meanwhile Garcia de Lerma died,
and the Dr. Infanta remained there. During his time not
only was no increase made in the extent of the province, but
it suffered diminution, many Spaniards leaving it, who had
come there as settlers. Afterwards Don Pedro de Lugo
arrived as governor, with a good force and a fleet; and he
sent his son Don Alonzo to a province called Ramada, which
is on the coast towards Cabo de la Vela, where there were
two or three chiefs more pacific than the others. The land
was plain, and rich in gold, and they always gave some of it
to the captains who went there. Thence Don Alonzo went
to the snowy mountains, and there captured a rich chief,
with a quantity of gold, with which, without doing more in
that land, he returned to Santa Martha.

After being there some days he embarked in a ship, on
the day before the gold was to have been melted down, that
each man might have his share, without his father knowing
anything about it, and went to Cuba with all the gold.
There he melted it, and went on to Spain. The other people
who remained behind went with the licentiate Jimenez to
the great river, some by sea and others by land. Five
brigantines were lost at the mouth of the river, but another
went on to Carthagena. Jimenez, who went by land,
ascended the river until he arrived at Bogota, where he
formed a settlement. This province of Santa Martha was
not very populous. The wind blows from the north and

north-east during the greater part of the year, and therefore there is little rain, for when these winds blow it does not rain. There are many very good partridges of the size of doves, and the food of the people consists of maize and *yucas*. The sheep and cows that are raised in that land, are of the best breed in the Indies.

The Indians of that land have no ceremonies, nor do they worship anything except the figures they work in gold and in cloth, which have a resemblance to the devil.[1] Men and women go naked, like those of Carthagena.

In the province of Ramada, near the Cabo de la Vela, they have discovered pearl fisheries, to which certain men have gone from the islands of Pearls, to settle there.

On the death of the adelantado Don Pedro de Lugo, Geronimo Lebron was sent as governor to Santa Martha, and he went on to Bogota, as has already been said. On his return to Santa Martha he found that Don Alonzo de Lugo had arrived as governor, so he went back to his own house at Santo Domingo. Villafuerte, and the others who killed Bastidas, fled inland to the villages of the Indians, and wandered over wide tracts of land, but the Indians never injured them. On returning to Santa Martha, they were seized and sent to Santo Domingo, where justice was executed on them.

On my arrival at Panama I will send what remains to be told of these provinces, and the dates of events that are wanting.

[1] See page 3.

FINIS.

INDEX.

Candia, Pedro de, lands at Tumbez, 46
Cannibals arrive at Paris, 40
Capucigra, Indian chief, 44
Careta, province of, 8 ; Cacique, 8 note
Carthagena, salt on the Isla Fuerte, 3; affairs of, 80
Castañeda, licentiate, governor of Nicaragua, 39
Catellez, province of, 76
Cenu, 27 (see Zenu)
Chame, near Panama, 25, 28
Chasquio, province of, 74
Chepo, 28
Chepobar, 28
Chiman, 28
Chiriqui, 37
Chiru, chief of a province near Panama, 25, 26, 29
Chochama, province of, 40
Chucheres, a remarkable tribe of Indians, 23
Ciaman, river of, 65
Codro, the astrologer, warns Vasco Nuñez, 21 note
Coiba, province of, 11, 25, 29, 31, 75
Colon, Admiral, discoverer of the coast of Tierra Firme, 6
Comogre, province of, 10, 27, 28
Contreras, Rodrigo de, governor of Nicaragua, 39
Cueva, province of, 11, 19, 23, 29, 31, 40, 75
Cutatara, chief of Paris, destroys a race of cannibals, 40 (see Paris)
Cuzco, entered by Soto and Almagro, 52 ; besieged by Inca Manco, 53 ; Pizarro sends succour to, 53

Darien, Pedrarias lands at, 3 ; Pizarro with the remnant of Ojeda's followers, settles at, 4 ; condition of the colony at, 6, 7 ; abandoned, 32
Dominica, island of, 2 and note

Escoria, a chief at war with Nata, 25; war between Paris and, 30
Espinosa, the Licentiate Gaspar de, accompanies Pedrarias, 2 note ; appointed to try Vasco Nuñez, 22; goes by land to Panama, 23; commands an expedition by sea to Nicaragua, 24; expedition of, to the westward, 28; account of, 29

note; in partnership with Pizarro, 43 note ; death of, 59 ; account of, 59, note; Belalcazar hears of death of, 62
Enciso, The Bachiller, goes to Darien with Pedrarias, as alguazil mayor, 2 note
Estete, Martin, sent by Pedrarias to Manalca, 38

Federman reaches Bogota, 77

Gallo, island of, 44, 45; heroic resolution of Pizarro at, 45; account of the Indians on the coast opposite to, 76
Garavita, Francisco, sent by Vasco Nuñez to Cuba, 18; to be sent to Acla for news by Vasco Nuñez, 21 note
Gorgone, island of, 45
Guanacaba Inca, 49, 57
Guanate, province of, alligators in, 39
Guarage, 30
Guatemala, conquered by Alvarado, 79; account of, 79-80
Guazcar Inca, brother of Atabalica, 49

Heredia, Pedro de, governor of Carthagena, 80; imprisoned by Badillo, 81 ; governor of Santa Martha, ib.
Hernandez, Francisco, settles Nicaragua, 36; revolts against Pedrarias, 36 ; beheaded by Pedrarias, 37
Huista, province of, discovered by Espinosa, 24
Hurtado, Benito, founds a town called Fonseca, 37

Incas (see Yncas)
Indians on the isthmus, treatment of, 7; manners and customs of, 13-17; mode of dispensing justice, 13; laws of, 13; superstitions of, 14 ; method of performing obsequies of the dead, 15; weapons of, 17; division of, in repertimiento, 23; remarkable tribe of, called Chuchures, 23; of Nicaragua, customs of, 33 ; of Popayan, revolt of, 61; dress of, 66; conversion of, by Andagoya, round Popayan and Lili, 67-74; warlike Indians of Apirama, 78 ; of Santa Martha, 80

LONDON : T. RICHARDS, 37, GREAT QUEEN STREET.

For EU product safety concerns, contact us at Calle de José Abascal, 56–1°,
28003 Madrid, Spain or eugpsr@cambridge.org.

www.ingramcontent.com/pod-product-compliance
Ingram Content Group UK Ltd.
Pitfield, Milton Keynes, MK11 3LW, UK
UKHW012339130625
459647UK00009B/388